PAINTED ILLUSIONS

A creative guide to painting murals and trompe l'oeil effects

PAINTED ILLUSIONS

A creative guide to
painting murals and
trompe l'oeil effects

TIM PLANT

WARD LOCK

To Mother and Father,
who gave us everything.

© Text and drawings Timothy Plant 1988, 1991
© Photography Ward Lock Limited 1988, 1991
First published in Great Britain in 1988
by Ward Lock Limited, Villiers House,
41/47 Strand, London WC2N 5JE

First paperback edition 1991

A Cassell imprint

Photographs by Jon Bouchier
Text filmset/set in 11/12 Garamond Light
by Dorchester Typesetting Group Ltd.
Printed and bound in Portugal by Resopal

British Library Cataloguing in Publication Data
Plant, Timothy
     Painted illusions: a creative guide to
     painting murals and trompe l'oeil effects.
     1. Trompe l'oeil painting—Technique
     2. Mural painting and decoration——
     Technique
     I. Title
     751.7   ND1390

ISBN 0-7063-7011 2

CONTENTS

INTRODUCTION 6

1 THE NATURE OF *TROMPE-L'ŒIL* 18

2 SELECTING AN AREA TO PAINT AND SUBJECT MATTER 26

3 PREPARING TO PAINT 38

4 PAINTING THE WALL 46

5 DIFFERENT TYPES OF *TROMPE-L'ŒIL* AND HOW TO PAINT THEM 58

6 THE WORLD BEYOND THE WALL 72

7 LIVING FORMS IN MURAL PAINTING 90

8 *TROMPE-L'ŒIL* DEVICES ON THIS SIDE OF THE WALL 102

9 THE PAINTING OF AN INDOOR MURAL 110

EPILOGUE 118

APPENDIX: PITFALLS TO BE AVOIDED AND OTHER PRACTICAL HINTS 122

ACKNOWLEDGMENTS 126

INDEX 127

INTRODUCTION

Painting murals is not just a pleasant pastime. It is an art form about as old as humanity itself. For the past 32,000 years, the artists who painted on walls have often been leading innovators in the pictorial arts. After the grand epoch of patronage in Italy, the art of mural painting went into decline. Now it seems to be coming back. A brief outline of this history should provide the reader with a useful perspective for the chapters which follow.

The art of mural painting is said to be enjoying a vogue. It has done so before – at different times and places, in different cultures, for different reasons – ever since the cavemen first decided to paint images of beasts on their cave walls. In fact, because of the way it developed in their hands, the painting of murals can probably be counted as the first truly creative activity of mankind.

Whatever their reason for doing it, whatever their skill, the cavemen were in effect amateur painters, and it is primarily to the amateur painters of today that this book is addressed. In earlier times – the Italian Renaissance for instance – there were studios where artists were specifically taught how to paint on walls, so that they could earn their living by it. But today there is no such thing – we have all had to teach ourselves! That is the main reason why I believe that this book can be of interest and instruction to the amateur painter who wishes to have a try. I also hope it might be useful to those who are fond of art and have studied a bit of art, but who have somehow never found a way to channel their interest – those who would like to paint but who have lacked a reason for painting. This is a real dilemma, but a very wasteful one, because it prevents people from doing what they might otherwise be able to do.

Painting a wall can be an exciting challenge. It is fun. It does require a certain amount of courage, and some careful planning and consideration, but it can indeed satisfy one of the deepest of human needs – to make something with our own hands. Not to forget that it can also provide an interesting and amusing complement to a scheme of interior or garden design.

There are a number of practical problems in creating a work of art on something larger than a piece of paper, and they will be dealt with in full, as clearly as possible. But what I also hope to do in the course of this book is to convey my own experience of painting murals, in terms of the real driving forces behind it: the feelings and affections, the intuitions and associations of ideas that give rise to subject matter and influence composition. These of course are vital ingredients of a work of art, just as much as the painting skills themselves.

The phenomenon of mural painting is probably too old and varied ever to have been treated in its entirety by one person in a single book. An art historian would probably see no reason for doing it. But I as an artist, not as an art historian, would like to start by considering briefly what has been done in the past, commenting on it from the artist's point of view.

30,000-10,000BC   Tens of thousands of years before the birth of Christ, the cavemen of the Early Stone Age realized that they could make the likeness of things on flat walls. How did it happen? Appropriately, the earliest known work is an image of hands on a cave wall. We shall never know exactly how it was started, but we can imagine someone leaning against the side of a cave and leaving the imprint of a hand on its sooty surface . . . then trying it again.

Magical or ritualistic reasons are offered for the paintings of animals on the walls and roofs of caves, suggesting perhaps a primeval sense that they would bring fortune in hunting, and fertility to the herds. The cavemen showed beyond doubt that a creative instinct lies deep in our nature. They gave priority to their art in a harsh world, where other more practical things might have seemed to be more important. They made experiments and developed their art. They worked in different media, and in colour. They used the natural shape of the rocky surface to enhance their work. And in their use of crosshatching and the foreshortening of their figures, they showed a remarkable aptitude for the representation of form.

The art of the cavemen had its golden age like so many other forms of culture, and then went into decline. But what is interesting about its later manifestations, during the Middle Stone Age, and exonerates them completely, is that we see here for the first time what may be regarded as the central challenge to artists of all ages – the representation of the 'human figure in action'.

10,000-3,000BC

The painted image of the human figure in action, and indeed in the sublimest passive state, can be said to have had its first thorough development in the murals of ancient Egypt. Although this art is not associated in any way with the classical or European traditions familiar to us, and is therefore about as foreign as any art can be, it is still remarkable for the clarity of its images and its narrative quality. We may not understand the signs and symbols of the hieroglyphs that accompany the paintings, but when we see those busy little rows of figures at work, and the serene grandeur of their patrons seated in state, we can hardly fail to be affected by them. We feel sympathy for those men of ancient times, as well as for the artists who depicted them. This proximity of the unintelligible hieroglyphic symbol, or 'picture writing', and the painted human figure in Egyptian art, certainly offers us the best example of the power and value of the straightforward painted image, able to communicate meaning and to stimulate affection in ordinary people across a wide gulf of culture and time.

The Egyptians, like the cavemen, believed in the magical power of painted images, but they also had a strong sense of the eternal. A flawless representation on the walls of a tomb provided the best repository for the soul in eternity.

The strong idiosyncratic quality of Egyptian art seems to have had strangely little artistic influence on the Greeks and Romans, whose presence in Egypt effectively broke its long, stable tradition. Little is really known about the pictorial art of the ancient Greeks, because so little remains, but mural painting came to prominence once again in the hands of the Etruscans, who flourished in central Italy before the ascendancy of Rome, and whose tomb paintings of rich men at their pleasure were distinctly Greek in style.

300BC-400AD

700-100BC

It was not until the Romans took up the brush, or in most cases immigrant Greek painters in the pay of Roman patrons, that mural painting finally came 'out of the tomb'! By now the painting of the human figure had reached a certain sophistication, and at this point it was supplemented by a most important innovation – landscape. Mural painting in Roman times was not done purely for ritualistic or funerary reasons; it was done for pleasure.

100BC-300AD

Wealthy and even middle-class families had murals painted on the walls of their houses and apartments so that they could enjoy them. Thus the mural was already an integral part of interior design. The Latin writer Pliny described the effect of a mural he had seen as that of looking out of a window at a landscape, not at a wall. The realistic representation of flora and fauna in mural painting reached a high level in their hands, reflecting the kind of enjoyment the Romans also derived from formal gardens and attractive rural scenes.

200BC-79AD
The Roman taste for mural painting and illusion is best illustrated by the examples at Pompeii, paradoxically preserved by volcanic ash when the town was destroyed by Vesuvius in AD 79. Rows of painted columns, or other architectural devices, made the surface of the wall appear to recede, providing the illusion of a three-dimensional space for painted figures or distant landscape scenes.

No one knows whether the ancients actually evolved a system of perspective for painting based on the single vanishing point for straight lines receding into the picture, as was evolved in the Renaissance, but the murals unearthed at Rome and Pompeii certainly suggest that the painters of the day had come pretty close.

300-750AD
After the decline of Rome and the advent of Christianity, the art of mural painting survived in western Europe and in the Byzantine world, but you might say that it went 'back into the tomb'. Inferior murals were painted on the ceilings of catacombs, or mass-burial vaults, and the importance of natural beauty gave way to a kind of religious symbolism in which the quality of the painted image was of scant importance. One redeeming feature of this dismal phase of art was the appearance of certain themes – the Madonna and Child; the Annunciation – which were later to become the subject of some of the best works of art ever produced.

Mural painting also flourished at this time, together with mosaic, in the churches of the Byzantine culture. But here again the value of natural truth and beauty, cherished in classical times, gave way to a rigid, schematic symbolism whose only function was to keep people on the straight and narrow. Various works of this kind were executed in Italian churches, in fresco and mosaic,

330-1453AD

1261-1453AD
during the early days of the Renaissance. A late revival in Byzantium itself, based on fresco rather than mosaic, saw a degree of liberalization of the former rigid norms, and this too had an effect on the development of western art. The Byzantine influence was particularly strong in the religious mural painting tradition of France.

c.1300AD
A reaction to the Byzantine tradition was heralded by a series of murals in the Basilica of St Francis of Assisi, based on the legend of St Francis himself. Giotto is said to have had a hand in these, and they effectively set the pace for large-scale mural painting throughout the coming years. One of the main features of Giotto's break with the past was that his representations were realistic. Unlike the figures in any art since the end of the Roman Empire, his were alive! His scenes were dramatic, and they

evoked an emotional response from the viewer. In short, they were fun.

Giotto and the Assisi school became the main focal point of artistic effort throughout a period in which the International Gothic style prevailed, and which saw the production of various large mural cycles in churches. But it was not until the arrival of Masaccio in the early fifteenth century that Giotto found his true heir. Rejecting the International Gothic style in favour of a grander, more naturalistic approach – as in his murals at the Brancacci Chapel in Florence for instance – Masaccio was famed

Italian flavour in a mural as a tribute to the land where this kind of art was largely developed.

c. 1425AD

for his scientific use of perspective, and the employment of light and shade in the pictorial construction of his figures.

1474AD

Illusion, or what we would call *trompe-l'œil*, is now seen again for the first time since the days of Pompeii, in the art of Andrea Mantegna. His narrative group portraits of the Gonzaga Princes of Mantua, on the walls and ceilings of their palace in that city, depict the various members of the family standing in space and leaning from balconies on the ceiling. The painted architectural structures which surround them effectively open the walls and provide a 'real' space for the figures to stand in.

c. 1500AD

Another of the most interesting products of this period was a series of domestic murals executed by artists of the Ferrara School, at the Palazzo Schifanoia in Ferrara, representing the court life of the ruling Este family in an astrological setting. This, together with Mantegna's work in Mantua, must be one of the first great examples of secular mural painting during the Renaissance.

c. 1485AD

1505AD

Leonardo da Vinci's ill-fated mural in the dining room at the Convent of S. Maria delle Grazie in Milan – the *Last Supper* – though a masterful catalogue of human action, posture and emotion, as well as an exercise in compositional perfection, is probably as well known for the fact that the medium he used to paint it was a disaster. Shunning the standard technique of fresco, he used an incompatible mixture of substances which made it start to decay soon after it was completed. His other great mural, the *Battle of Anghiari* at the Palazzo Vecchio in Florence – a powerful commentary on the madness of war in which a writhing mass of warriors and their horses were shown in mortal combat – would doubtless be one of the leading masterpieces of the Italian Renaissance had it survived.

c. 1510AD

c. 1510AD

The art of mural painting in the sixteenth century was of course dominated on the one hand by Raphael, with his Vatican Rooms, strongly influenced by a revival of interest in the classical art of Rome. Notable among these is a massive composition with a deep perspective, in which the philosophers of the ancient world are related to the Fathers of the Church. On the other hand, the works of Michelangelo on the Sistine Chapel ceiling probably defy mere verbal description, and require no introduction as a sheer explosion of creative effort on an almost superhuman scale.

c. 1640AD

Following a period of political turmoil and artistic bewilderment, which gave rise to the style of Mannerism, the Baroque Age produced a distinguished mural painter in the person of Pietro da Cortona, who seems to have been the first to specialize in the art of illusionist painting, or *trompe-l'œil*, on a grand scale. Among his greatest triumphs is the ceiling at the Barberini Palace in Rome, in which his figures actually seem to float up and down through an imaginary opening to the sky. After looking up at that one for a while, the viewer is rather glad to find that he still has the ground beneath him. The importance of the Baroque Age to the art of mural painting lies in its almost theatrical approach to architecture, and in its vision of architecture, sculpture and painting as an inseparable whole. It can also be regarded as a golden age in the art of ceiling painting.

What is generally seen as the great epoch of Italian art, in which the mural played such a dominant role, appropriately came to an end with one of the most able muralists of all – Tiepolo. He offered the richness of Venetian colour in a Baroque setting, adroitly combined with a rare mastery of perspective. In a strange, but thoroughly effective mixture of realism, illusion and fantasy, he transformed his favourite subject – Cleopatra – into a Baroque society beauty, and at the Palazzo Labia in Venice we see Anthony and Cleopatra virtually stepping out of the picture into the room. In his later masterpiece on the walls of the Kaisersaal and staircase at the Archbishop's Palace in Würzburg, the Baroque ideal of architectural and pictorial unity is admirably fulfilled.

1745AD

1750AD

France in the meantime had become an important centre of the arts, and here too mural painting had its part to play, though apparently never to the same extent as it had in Italy. Lebrun's Great Staircase at Versailles, later destroyed, was a prime example, and the tradition of the baroque *trompe-l'œil* ceiling was perpetuated by Antoine Coypel in such places as the Chapel at Versailles.

c. 1675AD

c. 1710AD

The relative frivolity of the Rococo period found no place for the more ambitious kind of mural, as the Baroque Age had done. It was a period of undemanding decoration, characterized by a taste for monkeys in fancy dress, arabesques and chinoiserie.

Throughout history, the best artists were often produced at times when there was no clear distinction between the artist and the craftsman. Typically, in ancient Greece, Egypt and Renaissance Italy, the painter was not treated as a special person, a 'creative genius' or some kind of guru set apart from the artesan or mason. Like everyone else, he learnt his skill the hard way, by means of apprenticeship according to an established set of rules. After the French Revolution and its ramifications in Italy, there was a decline in the traditional system of patronage, and the artist was, so to speak, thrown back on his own resources, which meant fighting for survival in a competitive market. This situation largely prevails today. It has probably had a greater effect on the art of mural painting than on other forms of art, since, in professional terms, murals were always done in other people's houses, and had to be commissioned. Sculpture and canvas painting lent themselves readily to a market in which the art dealer and the commercial gallery led the way.

This must be a main reason, though perhaps not the only one, why the mural painter of today is something of a Cinderella figure, excluded from that odd, dubious phenomenon called the 'Art World', and having to find his own way in an age of lost tradition.

The painters of the neo-Classical and Romantic movements which followed the upheavals of the Revolution were apparently not in the habit of painting murals, and the styles of painting adopted by the Impressionists and the various modern schools hardly suited the needs of interior design.

The overpowering influence of the modern, non-figurative schools of painting reached such an incredible level in the

The dining-room window of this villa in central Italy faces a narrow passageway. A sense of space and distance was created in this narrow place by painting a wine cellar on the facing wall. The composition included a painted arch to open up the wall, the wine cellar beyond, an imaginary window on the far side, and a view of the actual landscape on the far side of the building (see page 55). The dining room itself – on this side of the real window – has flowering Umbrian landscapes on its four walls, in a surrealistic setting of stone steps and terraces, with the glass roofs of conservatories floating in a clear sky.

course of this century that some art students actually felt inhibited if they wished to paint the human figure in its natural form. Perhaps the true value of an artistic movement is inversely proportional to the amount of pressure it puts on its artists to conform! Anyway, the happy outcome of such an unpleasant situation is that today we have no schools, no doctrines, no prevailing styles. Artists are truly freer to do what they want than they have ever been before. The current popularity of the mural has grown up in this atmosphere, largely because of a vibrant and ever-increasing interest in home improvement and interior design.

Partly because of this age of artistic freedom, I experienced some difficulty in arriving at suitable subjects to paint in my first murals, but since I was always painting for other people, my work was conditioned to some extent by their taste. In England there has always been a strong preference for landscape and garden scenes, often without the presence of the human figure. My early efforts were therefore devoted largely to experimenting with the various components of landscape and garden design, and fitting them into suitable *trompe-l'œil* 'frames'. This required considerable ingenuity in a lot of cases, because, unlike the surfaces normally used for painting murals in the past, I had to work on surfaces which were not designed for painting. I enjoyed this part of the challenge, and the results were all the more surprising. I soon began to realize that *trompe-l'œil* used in this way had something of the potency of a theatrical illusion or a conjuring trick, but I also felt that it had to be more than this. Optical trickery and illusion by themselves were not enough – to achieve their true value they had to be made an integral part of a coherent work of art.

There was no longer any need to glorify the owner of the property and his family, nor to express philosophical or religious ideas, as there had been in the past. My immediate aim was thus to please the eye and stimulate the imagination. Whereas many artists in the twentieth century have shut themselves in the studio and spent their time performing experiments in form and texture under 'laboratory conditions', to be sold by galleries to people they would probably never meet, my job was to produce slightly more than a mere image of reality – a work that not only embellished its real location, but actually changed it.

Transferring the creative act from the secrecy of the studio into the front line of everyday life was a major challenge, not least because of the element of performance it entailed. People were constantly watching me as I wobbled on my ladder, and few could resist some kind of participation in the process, constructive or otherwise. Their presence was thus a significant part of the reality on to which my work was being grafted, and by the time it was finished they were a great deal more intimately connected with its production than if they had just gone out and bought a picture.

The eventual introduction of the human figure into my works naturally added to the theatrical flavour of the illusion, and I had to try and establish some sort of criteria for its presence in works of this kind. That is a matter we shall deal with later.

The shape or location of certain painting surfaces did not lend itself to an entirely realistic construction. Because of this, elements of surrealism began to find their way into the picture, by which I mean realistically painted, recognizable elements outside their normal locations in nature. The need to combine the real appearance of *trompe-l'œil* with the surreal appearance of these other elements in the work permitted a further step into the realm of fantasy, a step which had to be taken lightly, because of the need for them to complement one another in a convincing, stimulating manner, instead of creating an atmosphere of confusion.

From beginning to end mural painting is a constant process of development, in which certain changes may be required. These physical and human conditions of the job may appear to put limits on the artist's freedom, and in a way they do. But whether one is faced with a window in the painting surface or a client with a devouring passion for butterflies, one should always try to respond in a positive way to such points of departure. Anyone who paints a mural must do this, and I believe that the truly inventive spirit may in the long run have a better chance to develop under these conditions than in the subjective world of total artistic freedom, which has been so highly valued in our own time.

CHAPTER ONE

THE NATURE OF TROMPE-L'OEIL

The name is modern, but artists have been painting trompe-l'œil, *or optical illusions, for a very long time. Fine examples are to be seen at the excavated city of Pompeii. But what exactly is* trompe-l'œil, *and how does it differ from the more usual kinds of painting? How can it be used as a vital part of modern mural painting?*

*T*rompe-l'œil is a French term meaning 'trick the eye'. Technically, any painting or drawing which contains an illusion of depth – for example, a view down a street – could be called *trompe-l'œil*, because it literally tricks the eye into seeing a thing in depth instead of halting on the flat surface. But this is not what is generally accepted as *trompe-l'œil*, because we expect to see depth and perspective in a normal painting or drawing. *Trompe-l'œil* is the use of images painted in perspective in places and situations where we might not expect to find them. A famous case is the painted illusion of a violin hanging on the back of a door at Chatsworth. The element of surprise in this adds to the impact of the image, and makes it seem all the more real. but *trompe-l'œil* need not be confined to mere gimmickry of this kind – used in conjunction with ordinary painted themes it can become one of the most vital elements in a work of art.

Because of their nature, *trompe-l'œil* images are normally painted on walls and ceilings rather than on canvas. Hence the term *trompe-l'œil* has often been wrongly used to describe all kinds of mural painting. It is quite possible to paint an elaborate mural which contains no *trompe-l'œil* at all.

Unlike a framed picture hanging on a wall, surrounded by empty space, a mural as often as not fills the wall and, in a manner of speaking, makes it disappear. In certain cases, a large painted composition on a wall can fit comfortably into its surroundings without the help of any linking illusion. In other cases, the actual structure of the environment can be extended or modified in paint, so that what is real – the architecture and the decor of a room, or a garden wall for instance – becomes part of the painting itself and in turn makes the main body of the work much more a part of its surroundings than it would otherwise be. Effects of this kind are what I normally mean when I use the term *trompe-l'œil*.

A painted landscape in a frame is a decorative object which has one kind of effect, but if the painting is taken down and the artist paints the same scene on a larger scale through a pair of painted french windows, it has a completely different kind of effect. It is now much more a part of the room in question, and the room is much more a part of it! *Trompe-l'œil* used in this way effectively blurs the edges between the real world and that of illusion, and forms a bridge between them.

In the course of the book I shall be describing the various kinds of *trompe-l'œil* image which can either be painted alone, as individual decorative features in a room or garden, or as part of a larger composition containing what you might call a 'normal' painted theme – a landscape or a figure for example, or even a piece of abstract painting.

But the various kinds of *trompe-l'œil* device – as I use them – generally fall into a number of simple categories, depending on their position in the composition. Although I shall be going into detail about the different kinds later on, I think it would clarify the situation if I give a brief description of them at this stage, in order to provide a general view of the whole subject right from the start.

Below: *The different effects of* trompe-l'œil *and ordinary frame.*

OPENINGS IN WALLS

One of the most useful and effective *trompe-l'œil* devices is the illusion of an opening in the painted surface itself. This normally takes the form of a window or an arch, a doorway, a pair of french windows, a colonnade, or even a jagged edge left by fallen masonry.

Far left: A good starting point is some sort of opening in the wall. Left: The illusion of a bay window gives an added sense of space. Above: The illusion is enhanced by painted structures immediately beyond the wall.

EXTENSIONS OF THE EXISTING SPACE

Rather than simply making an opening in an existing wall to see something through, we can instead make the wall – or part of it – seem to disappear and re-appear further away or at a different angle, thus giving the idea of a larger space. A typical example of this would be a painted continuation of the roof beams of a conservatory, either in a straight line or radiating from a central point to give the idea of a curved extension of the conservatory. The illusion of a bay window is another case of this. Instead of placing a window in the flat wall, we can use perspective to create the illusion of a recess in the wall containing the bay window. In this way we again achieve that often vital extension of space required in a room.

TROMPE-L'ŒIL BEYOND THE WALL

A painted opening in the wall such as an arch or a french window often requires some sort of complementary structure beyond it, in order to make the whole illusion seem architecturally plausible, and indeed to increase yet again the sense of immediate living space, this time beyond the wall. Obvious painted structures which come to mind in this case are terraces, balconies, patios, flights of garden steps, corridors, porches and covered colonnades. These really are a part of the *trompe-l'œil* structure rather than the composition proper, since by their proximity they appear to be an extension of the 'real world', not simply an architectural item in a purely imaginary scene.

TROMPE-L'ŒIL THIS SIDE OF THE WALL

Many astonishing effects can also be achieved in that narrow layer of magical space which lies against this side of the painting

Above: *A painted gazebo on the walls and ceiling of a small enclosed landing forms a suitable* trompe-l'œil *frame for a rural scene.*

Opposite: *Plants go well with paintings. Here the 3-D in the picture is enhanced by rich conservatory growth. But the cat was unimpressed.*

Above: *Special effects can be created in the 'magical' layer of space on this side of the wall.*

surface. Painted illusions of curtains, architraves, mouldings, etc., are of course a necessary adjunct to the windows or other openings which we may already plan to paint. Purely ornamental drapes painted against the wall, with their relevant shadows, can be a highly decorative item. An image of shelves with books and other objects recessed into the wall is an effective form of *trompe-l'œil*. On one occasion I 'inserted' into the wall a cupboard with leaded glass doors and a service of crockery inside. Painted illusions of mirrors with reflections of the room in question, wall brackets, and even framed pictures apparently hanging on the wall can on occasion suit a particular requirement. Sundry items hanging on hooks or leaning against the wall can greatly add to the lifelike aspect of a mural composition. A typical example of the latter was a hay-loft I recently painted high on the outside of a building with the illusion of a ladder reaching up to it from the ground, plus of course the all-important shadow cast by imaginary sunlight, which created the impression of distance between the ladder and the wall.

The list of possibilities is endless, but one thing is certain – the *trompe-l'œil* image painted on a wall or ceiling very rarely fails to amuse and delight. Perhaps because of the fact that its subject matter is generally so much closer to everyday life than the subjects of ordinary painting – almost tangible you might say – people find the intimacy of this kind of art attractive.

The painting of illusions in perspective has a very long history – it dates back to Pompeii. People who knew little of science, and seemed to have no ordered system of perspective, used their natural ingenuity and imagination to create illusions of depth for their own pleasure. It sometimes surprises me that this approach to decoration – with its funny tongue-twister of a name '*trompe-l'œil*' – has not already become a much more central part of the artist's repertoire today.

TROMPE-L'ŒIL ON CEILINGS

Some of the most celebrated works of art containing *trompe-l'œil* have been painted on ceilings. One or two of them were mentioned in the Introduction. Any work of art painted on a ceiling automatically contains an element of sensation which a painting on a wall does not have, merely because we have to look up to see it, and our sense of balance and proportion – hence of reality – is slightly altered by the act of tilting the head backwards. An element of vertigo is introduced, and this can help to stimulate the imagination.

The normal function of *trompe-l'œil* painting on a ceiling is of course to make the ceiling look higher, or to open it to the sky, if not to make it seem to disappear altogether. The great ceiling painters of the past often produced massive vertical extensions of the monumental buildings they were working in, with a high level of precision and detail. The ceilings they painted on were often high already, and, as with all *trompe-l'œil*, this distance from the viewpoint added to the effectiveness of the illusion.

Today's ceilings tend to be lower, and no one is going to try and paint the Gateway to Heaven at this stage! But in certain circumstances there are fairly simple devices which can be used to create an enchanting 'open' effect on ceilings. These can either be painted alone, or in conjunction with themes to be developed on adjacent walls. The most simple and obvious of these would be a series of beams across the ceiling, covered in climbing plants – to create a pergola effect – with the sky overhead. Another viable solution would be a stone parapet on columns round the top of the walls, as an introduction to a continuation of the sky across the top with birds and clouds. The illusion of a tented roof made of striped canvas can produce a most attractive effect.

A slightly more complex illusion which I sometimes use, and which can only be effectively viewed from one side, is that of the curved dome of a gazebo made of cast iron, with its four supporting columns at the corners of the room. Since the top of the dome in this case must be off-centre, to give the illusion of a curved structure, it would be suited best to the kind of recess, or landing on a stairway, which can only be viewed from one side, otherwise the illusion will appear to be upside down.

You can see from this that the possibilities of *trompe-l'œil* are virtually endless. The initial problems to be solved are largely of a technical nature, i.e. getting the illusion to look right in the space in question. This is not a bad thing. On more than one occasion I have been stuck for a subject, and the need to solve this structural problem at the start has had the effect of introducing me to an idea for the painting. Once the brain starts working, it keeps working . . . and so the subject grows.

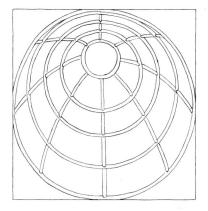

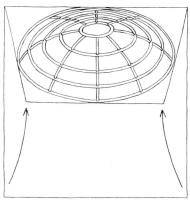

Top: *The centre is off-centre when viewed head on.* Above: *The dome appears curved when seen at ceiling-viewing angle.*

CHAPTER TWO

SELECTING AN AREA TO PAINT AND SUBJECT MATTER

Certain places cry out for some kind of decoration. It may be that ordinary pictures would seem out of place, or we simply haven't got the right ones, so that painting the wall itself becomes an attractive solution. Here we examine the wide range of paintable surfaces in the average house, and start to consider the endless possibilities for mural composition.

Unlike canvases and sheets of paper, walls and ceilings come in all shapes and sizes, and they are permanently located in many different kinds of environment. So, if we are going to paint a wall, or part of a wall, the first thing we have to do is define the exact area we want to paint. We can for example choose to cover the whole of a given area, with or without *trompe-l'œil*. Alternatively, we can select a part of the wall in question and paint, say, a window or an arch to form the *trompe-l'œil* 'frame' of our picture. In this case we have to decide the size, shape and position of our opening in the wall.

An important factor in this decision will be the function the painting is to serve, for example the elimination of eyesores and ugly walls, the enhancement of architecturally beautiful surfaces, the use of *trompe-l'œil* compositions to open up small or claustrophobic spaces, and the correction of architectural imbalances. Another important factor will be the use to which a particular room is put. In this chapter we shall consider one by one the various places inside and outside the house where people are most likely to want to paint a mural. In each of these cases we shall also look at what you might call 'phase one' of the choice of subject matter.

One of the great advantages which the art of painting has over many other forms of creative activity is also one of its greatest problems: the choice is infinite ... what are we going to paint? This is a highly personal matter and tastes differ widely. Since it would be impossible to cover all the available options for each case, let's start by going through a rough guide to the subjects I would be inclined to paint in the various locations listed below, without going into detail. The finer details of composition will then be considered later. In certain cases these subjects and locations will obviously be interchangeable.

Below: *A facing wall surrounded by foliage; nearby foliage and features of the garden are continued on the wall.* Bottom: *Trelliswork with climbing plants enhance a* trompe-l'œil *opening.*

OUTDOORS
The Facing Walls of Distant Buildings

If the regularity or continuity of a garden is broken by the presence of, say, a garage or a potting shed, this can be restored in various ways, depending on the surroundings. If the facing wall of the structure is surrounded by a reasonable amount of foliage, it is probably best to paint the whole wall so as to be able to extend the foliage on to the edges of the wall and perhaps carry it over the top to form a natural arch. Other forms of vegetation present in the garden or compatible with it could then be introduced to give added interest.

Within the natural arch you could perhaps choose to paint a distant landscape beyond a painted continuation of certain elements present in the garden such as lawns, hedges, paths, steps, flower beds, etc. A point worth remembering is that the illusion of distance is nearly always an effective, stimulating device in mural painting. Hence the popularity of landscape subjects.

If the facing wall is highly exposed and cannot be effectively disguised, we merely have to improve it. In this case I would tend

  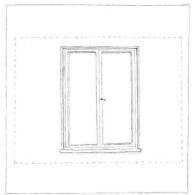

Far left: *Architectural and sculptural details with potted plants for the more formal garden.* Left: *A painted arch and trough with flowers can solve the problem of an asymmetrical wall.* Above: *The dotted line represents a suitable painting area on a close wall through a window.*

not to paint the whole wall but to create some kind of *trompe-l'œil* opening such as a curved stone arch, a garden gateway with wooden architraves, or even the illusion of a gap left by the fallen part of a ruined wall. In this case, rather than trying to make the wall disappear, we are actually making it part of the painting!

Once again, a safe bet for the contents of our *trompe-l'œil* frame is a distant landscape incorporating elements of the garden, to give the kind of romantic effect one seldom tires of. According to taste, and to the type of garden in question, we could instead paint the illusion of an alcove containing a stone statue, an ornament or a fountain, the bare sections of wall round this centre-piece being enlivened with painted trelliswork and climbing or potted plants.

The precise location of the kinds of *trompe-l'œil* opening mentioned above may be dictated by the shape of the wall in question, but in some cases it can be varied according to taste and successfully offset by counterbalancing items.

A garden is a continuous panorama of changing interest. The presence of a blank wall can interrupt this panorama and destroy its balance. Our aim in painting the wall must therefore be to restore the continuity of changing interest so that the wall fits into the garden, whether we make it melt into the background or turn it into a harmonious focal point in a position of prominence.

The Sides of Nearby Buildings to be Viewed Through a Window

Many windows have no view at all, because they either look out on to a passageway or the well of a house. Such confined spaces provide an ideal opportunity for the painting of murals. Since a painting of this kind is going to be viewed through a window, it already has an effective frame, and we have to take this as our starting point in choosing an area to paint. The average passageway is 1.5m (4ft) wide and if we paint an area about twice as wide as the window it should fill the visible area of the wall from most points of view.

Since the wall is very close to the window and we can see nothing but the wall, we are not faced with the problem of integrating our work into the surrounding scenery as in the cases above. We just want to make the wall disappear, and replace it with an image which will be altogether more pleasing on the eye.

Right: *The images go beyond the edges of the window to accommodate all angles of view.*
Far right: *A view into the well of a house; a suggestive, surrealistic view can open up a closed area.*

A simple but satisfactory way of doing this is to paint a finely gradated sky across the whole area, and set against it certain elements that will give the necessary notion of depth, such as close foliage and distant trees, skyline, birds in flight and scattered clouds. Please remember that at this stage we are only dealing with the painting area and general ideas for subject matter. In this kind of work we have to have a general idea about our subject before we can go into detail.

If the wall is further away from the window, so that more of it is visible in the arc of vision offered by the window, it is advisable to opt for some kind of *trompe-l'œil* structure which breaks the monotony of the wall, rather than trying to make the whole thing disappear. Since we are trying to reduce the atmosphere of confinement in, say, the well of a house, a feeling of openness and distance is again to be desired. This need not necessarily be a straightforward landscape or scene. Even if we use a realistic *trompe-l'œil* frame, a strong sense of openness and distance can be achieved by non-realistic means.

Various Parts of Garden Walls

If a garden is surrounded by the kind of wall which makes it seem like a prison yard, it is not necessary to paint the whole thing in order to improve the situation. A well-positioned decorative composition or *trompe-l'œil* opening in the wall will do a great deal to dispel the enclosed atmosphere of the garden. In choosing an area to paint we must consider the view from the house, from garden sitting areas, and of course the distribution of trees, shrubs etc., in the garden. As gardens of this kind are likely to be in town, a reasonable subject would be a typical town garden gateway with an attractive street scene beyond.

Enclosed Patio Areas

By their nature, patios are often built in areas next to houses, which means that they probably have high walls on one or more sides. These blank areas can be an overpowering presence, and thus lend themselves to a panoramic representation over the whole area incorporating features of the patio such as paved areas, low walls, urns, garden furniture, arbours, etc., in order to continue the feeling of patio beyond the wall.

Below: *A small garden with a high wall; the gateway provides that necessary breath of air.*
Bottom: *A patio dominated by a high wall; the patio is continued beyond the wall, leading to an open vista.*

Above and opposite: *A classic illusion of depth in this painted porch and colonnade beside an indoor pool. Heavy box beams across the ceiling provided the starting point for composition, and the half-dome is complemented by an illusion of mosaic on the floor. It was painted on a flat wall.*

Right: A conservatory with a large blank wall. An alcove with objects is set off by trelliswork and climbing roses, expanded at the top.
Far right: The end wall is painted as an extension of the wooden structure.

Conservatory Walls

The situation in a conservatory is often similar to that of the patio, since many conservatories have high dominating walls, and the same kind of solution may be applied.

Another appropriate solution is to cover parts of the wall with strips of trellis and climbing plants, potted plants painted close to the wall, and perhaps an alcove containing one or more decorative or utilitarian objects.

Depending on the structure of the conservatory, its wooden framework may be continued on the wall against a blue sky, either wholly or partly, together with climbing or hanging plants and ferns.

Walls Next to Swimming Pools and Sports Areas

Swimming pools and sports areas are often built with long bare walls beside them. A suitable form of treatment for such areas would be a row of simple Spanish arches, which need not extend the whole length of the wall, containing the warm kind of imagery which will both complement sun-drenched terraces and compensate for the cool swimming conditions of other climates.

INDOORS
Living Room

Below: A long wall by a pool. A tropical scene takes off the chill.

A painted wall in the main living area can provide a focal point of interest which brings the room to life. The protruding area above certain mantelpieces is an obvious area to paint, or the recessed areas on either side. Areas in relief such as these can either be treated in their entirety, or partially with the use of *trompe-l'œil* devices such as alcoves. An agreeable alternative is a flat painted border repeating patterns or schemes already existing in the room. A suitably discreet subject for an area like this would be a vase or urn of flowers situated in an alcove or against a natural background.

Other irregular surfaces which stand out or disrupt the appearance of a room, such as triangular sloping sections caused by the proximity of the roof of a house, or sections of wall not at right angles with the rest, can be turned to advantage as the basis of a painting.

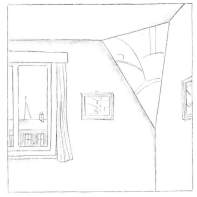
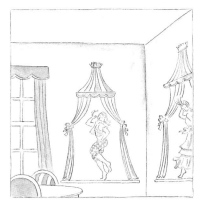

Dining Room

This is often the most formal room in the house and also the least used. The rather cold and unlived-in atmosphere of many dining rooms can be considerably improved by some kind of 'visual feast' on the walls. On more than one occasion I have been commissioned to paint all-round murals in dining rooms. But there is no need to go so far. A single wall or parts of different walls can go a long way towards creating the festive kind of atmosphere required at dinner parties.

Since eating is often associated with entertainment, one might choose to paint a number of colourful figures surrounded by decorative awnings. The figures can be simply done. They don't have to be Renaissance masterpieces, and a complete knowledge of human anatomy is not required, though a certain amount would help!

Bedroom

Built-in wardrobe doors are a favourite painting area in bedrooms. Existing wooden mouldings on the doors can provide a framework for painting. In their absence, we can either paint the whole area or create some decorative moulding, with or without further decoration outside it, as a framework.

In one bedroom containing six built-in wardrobes, each of which had a wide circular moulding in the centre, I painted a continuous river scene with waterfalls and rapids containing numerous real and legendary birds and beasts. But the atmosphere of the bedroom also lends itself to a more purely decorative approach. In another bedroom containing a suite of built-in furniture I painted in each of the surface mouldings a large floppy basket containing different kinds of wild flowers and grasses. Centre-pieces like this can be enhanced by the addition of angular corner bouquets containing the same floral species.

Murals in children's bedrooms are a firm favourite. Here of course we can depart from strict reality and refined taste, to enter the world of childish fantasy. All the standard characters are well-known, and most can be reproduced from books and comics with relative ease. I personally prefer to invent my own, and have occasionally even reproduced the likeness of the said small person in their midst.

Far left: *A sitting room with protruding chimney breast, and a formal composition with a vase of flowers.* Left: *An abstract design exploits an odd corner.* Above: *Carnival figures in the dining room.*

Below: *A bedroom with moulded wardrobe doors. The decorative baskets are enhanced by corner bouquets.*

Above: *The end of a corridor in a large flat close to the Albert Hall.*

Opposite: *Doors can become a part of the painted scheme.*

Right: *A bathroom with plain walls. A scene with classical ruins and columns lend itself to the luxuriance of bathtime.* Far right: *A plain wall at the end of the corridor.* Trompe-l'œil *is most effective in this setting.*

Bathroom

The lack of decoration in many bathrooms and the inadvisability of hanging pictures there because of humidity makes the bathroom a strong candidate for mural or *trompe-l'œil* decoration. Bathtime is also a time of meditation, so the areas visible from the bath lend themselves readily to this form of treatment.

In my experience classical ruins with columns and broken arches seem to go down well in this environment, perhaps because of their association with the idea of Roman baths. Such a framework as this can be an attractive setting for a scene of antique tranquillity, painted either in colour or as if it were a stone frieze. And for some reason, I have always been strangely tempted to paint a volcano above the loo.

Halls, Passageways, Landings

These areas are not living areas but areas through which people pass. Yet the impression they create is important, and a painted illusion can be used effectively to remedy defects and improve first impressions. The obvious areas to paint in this case are the blank walls one finds at the end of halls, passageways and landings, especially as perspective and *trompe-l'œil* devices are very effective when seen at a distance down the hall.

One of my most difficult *trompe-l'œil* paintings from the technical point of view – at an Italian villa – was to transform a narrow box-like entrance into a wide hall with a vaulted ceiling. This was a complex operation and one would not be advised to try it. But the end of a hall is usually a convenient size to paint, and of all locations it is probably the one which most exclusively calls for straightforward *trompe-l'œil* treatment. An appropriate solution here would be to open a french window on to a balcony with wrought iron railings, as an introduction to a suitable kind of scene.

Ceilings

The ceiling of any indoor area can be painted, but this form of decoration is perhaps most popular in the bedroom and the dining room.

The main problem of painting on a ceiling is a physical one, namely that of keeping the hand steady above one's head with nothing to rest it on while painting. An artist who is not used to painting on ceilings will initially suffer from a stiff neck and a sore arm! But I found I got used to it quite quickly the first time I did it, and I also found it an excellent way of improving my muscle control in what I was doing. This improvement has definitely been valuable in painting less awkward surfaces as well.

I almost invariably use a lightweight aluminium step-ladder in good condition, as this offers easy mobility about the ceiling without blocking the view from the floor as a fixed platform would do.

I do not advise beginners to try to paint human figures on ceilings at the start – unless they are very determined (and a person who is very determined can do anything) – but sky and clouds can be a delightful form of decoration for the ceiling of, say, a bedroom, with perhaps some uncomplicated birds painted in flight.

Another popular theme, either alone or in conjunction with a blue sky plus clouds, is a floral motif with loops of foliage running round the outside of the ceiling or around the rose in the middle. The latter combination is often suitable in the dining room.

Above: *A floral motif is a delightful decorative device on ceilings.*

CHAPTER THREE

PREPARING TO PAINT

It is while we are doing sketches that we largely develop the idea for a painting. This is a most important phase. Detail and quality are not so important at the very start. Variety and experiment are what count at this stage. Once we are sure we have the right idea we can start to go into detail and produce a scale drawing.

So far we have dealt in generalities. Now it is time to consider the practical side of things, and to do this I shall take as an example the mural I happen to be painting at the time of writing this book. It is a mural on the outside of a plain building on a country estate in central Italy. The owners of the mansion from which this building is visible considered it to be an eyesore, and wanted some kind of distraction to reduce its ugliness. Hence the mural.

Spontaneity is considered a virtue by many contemporary artists. They have a point, and they work directly from their brain on to canvas. Masterpieces have been produced in this way, but my experience tells me that when we are working on a larger scale, on walls rather than canvases, one or more preparatory drawings make a successful result much more likely. In fact, every mural I have painted has been developed in miniature on paper before I have even considered touching the wall.

INITIAL SKETCHES

In many cases I have no clear idea at the outset what I want to paint. If so, I do two or three very simple initial sketches to get an idea of what impact the various subjects might have. These are often variants of the subjects I briefly described in the preceding chapter.

I start by doing a rough line drawing of the location, in this case the outside of the building where I now sit typing. I consider the various parts of the facing wall which offer suitable painting areas, and immediately identify the tall central section and the broad area towards the bottom of the steps. I seem to have a choice of two *trompe l'œil* solutions: either leaving the wall as it is and painting decorative items against it, or creating an opening in the wall with a vista through it. These initial alternatives form the basis of my two drawings, and I start to do simple sketches. At this stage they are not drawn to scale.

A useful time-saving device to avoid drawing the outline of the building twice is to attach the second sheet of paper to the first with paperclips, and trace the outline holding the papers against the window.

I use ordinary HB pencils sharpened to a long point and a good quality heavy watercolour paper with a slight grain, of the

Below: An outline of the available painting surface. Right: Twining stems give a feeling of growth. Far right: The climbing plant insinuates itself into various parts of the surface.

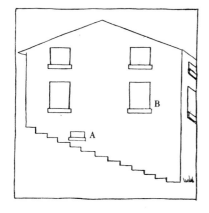

kind available in large sheets from nearly all art shops. I do not use cartridge paper nor the very expensive handmade papers from the Continent. Bockingford, Saunders and Cottman are all reasonably priced papers of superb quality. I cut the sheets into four equal pieces measuring about 40 × 55cm (16 × 22 inch), which is a good working size.

Many houses in that part of Italy are covered with large old wisterias, which at a certain time of year turn into vast cushions of mauve. It seems that this colour would go well with the pale ochre colour of the building, and being a climber the branches of the wisteria can be introduced realistically into the side areas of the surface.

Rather than one stem I draw two stems coiling round each other in irregular spirals. As a result these two interacting stems give a sense of movement, and we see in them the history of their growth. This is the kind of feature which brings a work of art to life.

The vertical and lateral sections of the wall are regular in shape, so it is important for the branches of our wisteria to follow them in a balanced but not completely regular way. This will help to distract from the monotony of the architecture which we are trying to get rid of. The abundance of flowers and small amount of foliage can then be distributed on the branches in a natural way.

Most of the buildings in this part of Italy are very old and built of rough-cut stones and mortar. I therefore choose to create the illusion that this very modern building has been built on the remains of an older building, and that the former masonry has been incorporated into the new structure.

Since we are in an agricultural community where all imaginable species outnumber human beings ten to one, I freely distribute their representatives on all available surfaces in a way which has been successfully employed by local folk-art sculptors for a long time.

In my first drawing everything is on the surface, this side of the wall. For the second of the initial drawings I choose a simple architectural extension of the kind referred to in the previous chapter. It is an arch leading to a stable with another arch on the far side. The same solution is applied above in the form of a hay loft, the latter being connected to the ground with a ladder. Since

Far left: Incorporated ruins link the modern building with ancient surroundings. Left: Local carvers have often included birds and animals in building structures. Below: Possible layout for a stable/loft mural.

the principles involved in painting these two openings are the same, I shall confine myself to describing how I create the stable.

The building is very plain, so I decide to incorporate a slight curve in the architrave of the front arch. This just manages to set off the squareness of the building and add some character. A more elaborate arch would be quite out of place. At the far end of the stable I draw a round arch of the kind present in certain older buildings on the estate, which I think complements the shallow arch at this end, and provides a suitable exit to that mysterious land 'beyond the wall'.

At the drawing stage the interior surfaces of the stable are to some extent a matter of speculation. Three lines give an idea of its shape, but they may have to be modified slightly at the painting stage to make it look as though the stable fits squarely into the building.

The landscape beyond the round arch is in fact a slightly impressionistic version of the existing landscape beyond the building, and the two horses are positioned to harmonize with the line of the existing flight of steps on this side of the building.

These initial drawings I do lightly in pencil with little or no shade, using an india rubber to make adjustments and alterations. It is the initial stage of the creative act, and now is the time to experiment and get the basic layout right. This can save a lot of work later on. Once I am satisfied with the layout, I go over my lines lightly with an artist's drawing pen (Joseph Gillot 404) and a neutral brown ink containing shellac, or more recently the kind of liquid acrylic colour which has just come on to the market, and which will not run when painted over with watercolour or wash. When the ink is dry, I rub out all the remaining pencil lines and am left with my desired layout. It is now ready for colouring, a process I normally start with pale watercolour wash, followed by stronger tones and shading where required, and finally perhaps some touches of coloured pencil to bring out highlights or create texture on the grained paper surface.

This drawing technique is quick and easy, and it suits my purposes well because I like to have a complete visualization of the composition in colour from the word go. There are doubtless other approaches and materials which would suffice as well. It is important to keep the sketches simple at this stage. Five simple sketches yielding the right idea are better than one elaborate

Below: *The complementary forms of two superimposed arches.* Right: *Three lines give the basic shape of the stable.* Far right: *The positions of the horses tie in with the steps, and the actual landscape behind the house is interpreted in an impressionistic way.*

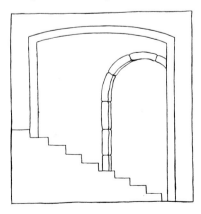

sketch which yields the wrong idea. In this case we have two. The more a work of art progresses, the harder and more painful it becomes to make major changes.

Don't be put off by the size or apparent complexity of this composition. Apart from the fact that it happens to be the work I am executing at the time of writing these words, I believe that it serves to illustrate many of the points I have made elsewhere in the book. In describing how I carry out a work of this kind, I hope that others will be able to apply the information in making compositions of their own, even on a more modest scale at first.

It is while doing our initial sketches that we hope to have the 'germ' of an idea. Its development comes next.

A mural in a small town garden can open it up and create a focal point of attention which enhances the other delights the garden has to offer. Here we have a surrealistic composition in a realistic trompe-l'œil *frame.*

SCALE DRAWING

In order to paint a smaller mural, measuring not more than about 3 × 1.5m (10 × 5 ft), I would probably not do a scale drawing at all if the initial sketch has turned out well. This is a matter of choice. But for larger works it is important, and for those who are not experienced it is a good idea to go step by step, as this will reduce the risk of getting into a muddle.

In this case I measure the distance between the small basement window (A) and the edge of the building. I then measure the distance between the bottom of the main window (B) and the ground. I take the largest of these numbers and divide it on my calculator by whatever number will give me a line that just fits on to my sheet of paper – the number I get is 23. I then divide the other dimensions by this number, and the result is a scale reduction which fills my sheet of paper almost exactly. In most cases of course the process is very much simpler, involving only the height and width of a much smaller surface.

I now have an exact reduction of the shape of my painting surface, and I can set about positioning my *trompe-l'œil* structure where it is actually going to be on the wall. In the initial sketch I was just interested in creating the idea; now it is a question of finding the best proportion and position to make it look a realistic part of the architecture. Having done this, I can now concentrate on filling in the composition with greater exactness and detail.

When the drawing is finished I use my calculator again to divide the width and height of the drawing itself into a number of equal sections, so that when the resulting squares or rectangles are transferred to the wall they will measure more or less 30 × 30cm (12 × 12 in). I draw the grid over my scale drawing lightly with a sharp pencil. This time I use a ruler.

PREPARING THE WALL

A careful preparation of an outdoor surface is important for three main reasons:
1. It will be easier to paint.
2. It will look better.
3. It will last longer.

If it is a brick wall, or a cement rendered wall in very bad repair, it is best to have it rendered by a professional workman. This is a fairly quick operation, but it is most important to wait until the cement is completely dry before starting to work.

If rendering is not required, all dirt, dust and loose paint should be removed, and good paint buffed up with sandpaper or an electric sander. All loose material should be removed from any cracks and ruptures in the surface. Holes and cracks should then be filled with a high quality smooth outdoor filler, using a spatula or small masonry trowel. If there are any deep cracks, they should be filled bit by bit, letting each layer dry thoroughly before the next is applied. When all the filler is dry, it should be rubbed down with sandpaper or an electric sander to make sure it is quite smooth. It is most important that the wall should be completely dry before any sealing agents are applied. Dampness beneath the surface is the worst enemy of paint.

Now give the entire painting surface one coat of Bollom's Neutralic Sealer or its equivalent. This is like a thick white matt paint, and it contains agents which neutralize the caustic substances in plaster and cement which make paint bubble and peel. This substance must be brushed on thoroughly with a wide flat brush, making sure that the sealer is evenly distributed all over the wall, then left to dry for twenty-four hours. The result is a perfectly stable white painting surface. If one of the transparent variety of masonry stabilizers is used instead, a coat of appropriate primer will be required afterwards. Any doubts about the suitability and use of such preparations can normally be resolved by asking the advice of a competent decorator. Exceptionally good and stable paint surfaces need only be sanded down, washed and perhaps given a coat of appropriate primer as a base for painting.

CAUTION: all tools, electric and otherwise, should always be used with care. Electrical tools must be properly wired, earthed and fused. If you are not sure about how to use them, get help from someone who knows. Keep all paints and sealers away from the eyes and mouth, and wash hands thoroughly after use.
The principles involved in preparing interior walls for mural paintings are exactly the same, except that we are normally dealing with plaster instead of cement, and there is a possibility of having to paint on lining paper or even existing wallpaper.

Bare plaster should be made good in the same way as described above, using a quality interior filler of the smooth variety. Like cement, the plaster must be thoroughly dry. In the case of new plaster, it should be allowed to shrink and crack, then filled, before commencing preparation. Neutralic sealer brushed evenly over the plaster surface will provide the ideal painting surface.

Ordinary lining paper can be used, but there is no real advantage in this, and it involves extra work and cost. The joins in the paper may also be visible when the work is finished. If lining paper is used, it should be coated with a white primer compatible with the kind of paints that are going to be used, i.e. oil or water based.

Existing non-gloss paintwork in excellent condition should be thoroughly sanded and treated with an appropriate primer as a base for painting. Existing lining paper, or an existing flat, matt wallpaper in very good condition, well fixed to the wall, may be primed in the same way and used as a perfectly adequate painting surface. Existing wallpaper in bad condition should be removed in the normal way, and a fresh start made on the bare plaster. Hardboard and wooden panels should be sized and primed for painting in the standard way.

The same safety precautions apply in this case, as always.

CHAPTER FOUR

PAINTING THE WALL

Now that the drawings are done and all the basic measurements made, it is time to go into action. Painting something larger than usual is very exciting, and a little nerve-racking too! Even after ten years, I feel a nervous shiver when I first put brush to wall. Work steadily, take it slowly at first, and remember – nothing is final. Everything can be developed and changed as the painting grows.

Having already drawn a grid on the scale drawing, you should now start to reproduce it on a larger scale on the wall itself. If the grid is only going to cover part of the wall, as in the case of my Italian mural, you must first of all position it.

To do this, measure the distance on the drawing between the edge of the mural and the right-hand corner of the building. Multiply this by the number you originally divided by (in my example, 23) to get the actual distance between the edge of the mural and the corner of the building. This edge of the mural is also the right-hand end of the grid. Using a plumbline you can now draw the right-hand vertical of the grid. In my example, the height is obtained by multiplying the height on the scale drawing by 23.

Position the vertical at the far end using the same calculations, and connect them across the top making sure that the line is horizontal. Now divide the width of the mural by the number of vertical sections, and mark the resulting spaces across the top.

For a plumbline, use a weighted string about 1m (3 ft) long, and draw your vertical lines lightly with a sharp pencil. In this way you divide the mural area into so many vertical sections of equal width.

Now divide the height of the mural by the number of horizontal sections, which you mark on the vertical lines. Connect these up with one another drawing straight horizontal lines, usually freehand but sometimes with a long ruler, and the end product is an enlarged grid on the wall.

Top row, left to right: *This line marks the right-hand end of the grid, also of the mural itself. The grid area must first be divided into a number of vertical sections, each of the same width. A short plumbline is best, the vertical line being drawn bit by bit.* Bottom row, left to right: *The equidistant marks on the vertical lines, and the horizontal connecting lines, can be done in groups of three or four at a time, to avoid too much moving about. The main structural lines are the first to go in. Only the main outlines are required at this stage. Smaller details can be located easily at a later stage.*

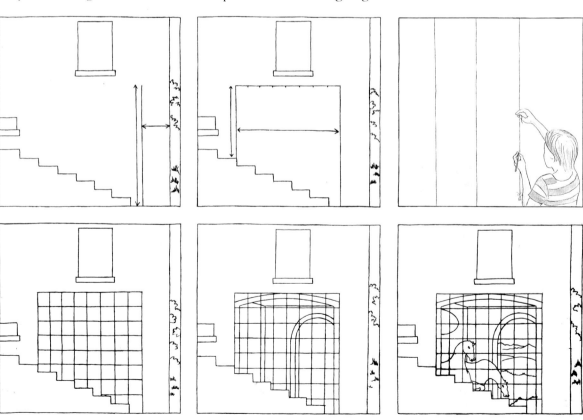

Never use magic markers or felt pens, because the dried ink permeates the subsequent layers of paint and is almost impossible to cancel out. The exact size and shape of the grid squares does not matter. The only thing that matters is that the number of grid squares is the same horizontally and vertically on the drawing and on the wall, and that they are all the same size. It is a good idea also to number the squares on the drawing and on the wall, alphabetically in one direction and numerically in the other, in order to avoid drawing things in the wrong squares when you are scaling up.

This may seem a laborious process, but the relatively small effort required really is worthwhile. Always try to draw your lines as straight as possible and to keep them light. Heavy lines show through.

At this stage, start transferring outlines from the drawing to the wall. There is no need to reproduce the entire drawing. The aim is to get things in the right places quickly and without a lot of trouble.

Once the main outlines are in place, the smaller details can be placed with ease during the painting phase. In this case the obvious lines to put in are the outlines of the front arch, the round arch on the far side, the three lines radiating from the corner of the stable, the oval window, the approximate profile of the horses, and the main lines of the landscape.

You have now reached an important stage in the proceedings, when you should stand back and take a long look at what you have done. Are these main lines of the composition, which looked all right on the drawing, compatible with the building and the landscape behind it from the point where most people are going to stand and look at the work? Most probably they are pretty nearly right, but they may need some adjustment, and now is the time to do it. There are three things to consider, especially in this particular case: is the left-hand wall of the stable going to be parallel with the walls of the house? Is the ceiling going to be horizontal? Does the horizon in my distant landscape correspond roughly with the real horizon?

Anyone who starts to paint a mural, even quite a small one, will soon realize that this activity is as much a sport as an art. It involves constant bending, stretching and contortions, and is an excellent way of keeping fit!

CAUTION: it is vital that you use a step-ladder which is in good condition and always place it firmly on the ground, before using.

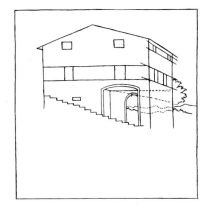

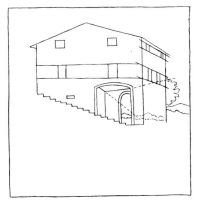

Top: *Do the structure and landscape fit properly into the world around them? Here they do.* Above: *Here they don't.*

MATERIALS

Murals have to be painted with permanent, hard-wearing materials, and this effectively limits us to two kinds of paint: oils and acrylics. The quality brands of these paints are so good and versatile that I hardly see any reason to consider the other traditional media, namely fresco, tempera and gouache.

Both oils and acrylics can be used on cement and plaster surfaces prepared with neutralic sealer, and each can be used on

the relevant surfaces prepared with oil and acrylic primer described in Chapter 3. The choice of which medium to use is to some extent a matter of taste, since the two kinds of paint have quite different characteristics, but there are also various practical considerations which weigh rather heavily when working on a larger scale. In practical terms the greatest advantages are offered by acrylics, and I would strongly recommend them for the following reasons.

Acrylics are water-based plastic paints. All you need for mixing and cleaning is a bucket of water. They dry as quickly as water, and when they dry a chemical reaction called polymerization takes place, which turns them into a kind of non-shiny flexible plastic coating on the wall. A lump of dry acrylic paint is rather like synthetic rubber in texture and behaviour. Once dry they are permanent and waterproof. They are opaque, which means you can paint over as soon as they are dry, normally after about two or three minutes, and you can paint over as many times as you like. Another very attractive advantage of acrylics is that they can be mixed with water to any consistency and the result is equally permanent. So, in extreme cases, we can squeeze the paint straight from the tube into a lump on the wall, or we can dilute it into the thinnest wash.

The advantages of oil paints, in my view, are almost all on the aesthetic side. Numerous artists who have been brought up on oils are unable to make the transition to acrylics because they feel that they lack the richness, depth of colour and, for want of a better term, 'sensual creaminess' of oil paints. These are the qualities which have made oil paints so popular over the ages, and they cannot be denied. But oil paints can be very messy, and they take a long time to dry. Colours containing a lot of white can take up to three days, which would lead to considerable delays in painting a mural.

Since oils take a long time to dry and possess that creamy fluid quality, they are ideal for blending colours into each other on the surface – for example when painting a sky which goes from blue, through white and yellow, to the reddish colour of a sunset. With acrylics it is harder to get a smooth transition, and they tend to leave a hard edge between one hue and another. Nevertheless, it is all a question of practice and learning to use one's materials. With careful blending and brushwork I think it is possible to get an equally effective result, and with acrylics you never get into those awful sticky messes where the only solution is to scrape everything off and start again!

Various acrylic additives are available in bottles and tubes to increase the flow of the paints and to help in creating textured effects, translucency, etc., when these things are desired.

All in all, it is probably fair to say that acrylics are to be highly recommended on larger surfaces, while on smaller ones, not larger than about 3 × 1.5m (10 × 5 ft), it is much more a matter of personal choice.

There are no matt oil varnishes that I know of, so oil murals would have to be left unvarnished or given a gloss varnish, which could lead to problems of glare and light reflection.

Opposite: An ugly modern building on an attractive country estate. While not exactly concealing the plainness of the building, the mural distracts attention from it, and has its effect in this way. A shallow curvature was chosen for the architraves of the stable and the hayloft, in order to offset the squareness of the building itself. Note the similarity of the painted stonework and the real stone on the windows.

Below: Oils (left half of picture) can be toned very softly. Leonardo called it 'dolce e sfumato' which means sweet and blurred. Acrylics (right half of picture) give a harder edge but can be equally effective.

Water-based matt acrylic varnishes are, however, available at reasonable prices in commercial quantities, from builders' merchants and paint suppliers, and they provide an excellent protective coating for indoor and outdoor murals. They dry quickly and are invisible when dry. I believe that in most cases it is better for murals to have a matt finish.

Before you start painting a mural, you should buy a selection of ordinary decorator's brushes ranging from 1 to 5cm (½ to 2 in) in width, to use for painting in the large areas. For the finer work, use round artist's hog brushes (bristle) of various sizes, and for very fine work use the soft round nylon brushes widely available in art shops.

As well as the normal tubes of artist's acrylic colours, buy a suitably sized can of top quality brilliant white matt emulsion paint for mixing. It is perfectly compatible with artist's colours, and much cheaper than titanium white in tubes for painting large expanses of surface. Artist's titanium white should be used only for painting in the more delicate details later. Use empty yogurt containers or plastic cups for mixing the larger quantities of paint, so that they can be kept from day to day if required, and an ordinary palette for the finer work.

Below: A typical distribution of shade in the corner of our stable. Bottom: Shading on the inside of the arch.

PAINTING

All the preparatory work has now been done, and the basic outline of the structure is marked on the wall. It is now time to start painting. Let us return to the Italian mural.

All the windowsills and architraves on the building are made of a local stone called *travertino*, which is a creamy white with many small holes in it. I therefore start by painting the front of the main arch the same creamy white, ignoring the holes for now.

I assume that the inside walls of the stable are whitewashed, but as they are in shadow they must be painted a shade of grey influenced by the colour of light reaching them indirectly, in this case the green of the grass and the pale sand colour of the driveway outside. So, the walls are to be a greenish grey with a hint of beige, the darkest parts being the corner of the ceiling, which receives the least light, then the upper edge of the far wall, then the upper edge of the left-hand wall.

Corners and edges are generally the darkest parts of walls, which gradually get lighter further away. You sometimes have to play around with your lights and shades in order to get the correct balance.

I now paint the inside surfaces of the front arch, the vertical one slightly darker than the front surface, and the one across the top darker still, because they are in relative degrees of shade. Note that the corner joint runs parallel with the left-hand edge of the ceiling, as in reality.

The sky is the lightest part of the painting, a pale sky-blue at the top fading down through white and yellow to a warm glow in the bottom right-hand corner. High wispy clouds of the kind shown offer a sense of remoteness and romance. The distant hills are painted in a pale cerulean blue, lighter and warmer on the right-hand slopes which are facing the light. The hills in the middle distance are deeper in colour, more of a grey-blue with hints of purple and green here and there, while the woods and fields between them and the foreground start to take on various shades of green. Scenery in the middle and far distance can look very cold if we are not careful. For this reason I include some strips of ochre and pink in the illuminated parts, denoting earth and cornfields for instance, and I make sure that some warm tints find their way into the parts in shadow.

The result of this effort is a slightly impressionistic rendering of the beautiful Umbrian landscape which actually lies beyond the building.

I now start to paint the horses, first of all by filling in the two areas occupied by their bodies, one with chestnut brown, the other with grey. This gives me an idea of the overall balance of the composition in terms of mass, tone and colour. It seems to be all right so far, which basically means that the work is not unduly dominated by one or more items, yet not so uniform as to be monotonous or nondescript. This is going to be a substantial but simple work, containing a few fairly strong components that are fairly well balanced and complement one another.

I now develop the parts of the horses' bodies exposed to light, using a paler version of each colour, darken the areas hidden from light, especially the creased areas around joints, and highlight the parts where the sheen of their coats would actually reflect the light. I also make sure that each has a positive expression on its face. Nothing is worse than dumb animals.

The horses are positioned to fit in with the existing flight of steps, one in a proud stance with a classically cropped mane, the other stooping with more mundane thoughts, such as food. The posture, attitude and expression of animals and human figures is an important matter which shall be dealt with later.

There are various ruined stone arches on the estate – it used to be a Benedictine convent in the Middle Ages – and I now paint in the round arch as a modern version of one of these. It must be darker than the stable walls, as this kind of arch was generally made of a grey igneous stone called *peperino*. This I reproduce with a uniform coat of the basic colour, which I then skim over with a 3cm (1 in) brush rubbed in a small amount of different greys containing brown, beige and blue respectively, so that different areas of the stonework are dominated by slightly different hues. This kind of stone has almost no grain in it.

When you are attempting this light skimming operation, try to use the inevitable roughness of the outdoor surface to create a mottled effect. Try also to keep it from becoming too uniform in texture, because stone surfaces are always changing. For variety you could take an old decorator's brush with some darker paint on it, rub off most of the paint on a cloth, then prod certain areas of the stonework lightly to create mottled areas of a different kind.

Note that the arch in the picture is made of stone blocks, which means that there are extra lights and shades on the edges between the blocks. Details of this kind will be dealt with later in

Top: *Light and shade distribution on the horses' bodies.* Above: *Stonework on the round arch. Light and shade on the edges of the stones give them a solid look.*

Right: *One of three painted arches in
an old Brazilian garden. A strong
colonial feeling was maintained in
this one. A hint of voodoo and
foreboding in the snakepot and
distorted staircase were my
unavoidable reaction to an odd,
almost uncanny atmosphere in the
house in question. The ghostly
presence of the boy soldier was a
character from the Brazilian classic*
Time and the Wind.
Far right: *What you see if you walk up
to the window pictured on page 15.
The contents of the cellar are typical
of the area: hams, bacons, garlic,
barrels and flasks of wine, a
traditional stone jar for olive oil, and
of course the proverbial cat. Note the
reflection in the window.*

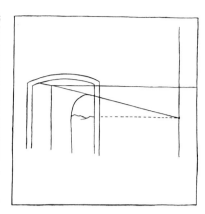

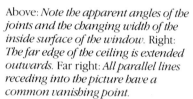

Above: *Note the apparent angles of the joints and the changing width of the inside surface of the window.* Right: *The far edge of the ceiling is extended outwards.* Far right: *All parallel lines receding into the picture have a common vanishing point.*

a chapter devoted to the creation of such effects. The inside surface of the round stone arch is much lighter, since it is exposed to sunlight.

In the top left-hand corner I insert the oval window made of the same volcanic stone, and through it I paint an indistinct arrangement of light and dark greens to suggest sunlight in foliage. I then insert the iron bars. Note how the inside surface of the oval window appears widest at the point where it is closest to being perpendicular to the line of vision, i.e. at the far end.

The ceiling rafters are made of rough-hewn chestnut wood, as in other buildings on the estate. The one on the left is virtually parallel with the left-hand edge of the ceiling, and the rest veer very slightly towards the vertical from left to right.

If perspective presents a problem, as in this case, you can do a simple experiment on paper with a pencil and ruler. Extend the edge of the ceiling out to the right so that the line would in reality run in front of the viewer. Then draw a line for the rafter which would run over the head of the viewer. On paper this one is vertical. Continue this vertical line downwards and extend the left-hand edge of the ceiling downwards until the two lines meet. This is the vanishing point, and it should be close to the level of the horizon. Now make a series of equidistant marks along the far edge of the ceiling where the rafters would end and draw a line from the vanishing point through each of these points across the ceiling. This gives the position of each rafter.

Perspective can be a bit puzzling at first, but it soon becomes second nature and such experiments cease to be necessary.

To return to the rafters in my mural, once their directions are established I paint them in a solid dark brownish grey, and add some subdued highlights on their downward facing surfaces to represent the grain of the wood. Again, the edges in contact with the ceiling are the darkest part, and this darkness must be reflected on the parts of wall and ceiling closest to the rafters. It is very often these areas of 'corner shade' which make things look real and stand out in relief.

The characteristic holes in the travertino stone vary in size. Some are very small and come in clusters. These I paint by prodding the wall lightly a number of times with the end of a 3cm (1 inch) decorator's brush containing a small amount of bluish-brown paint. The larger holes tend to come in erratic rows, and I

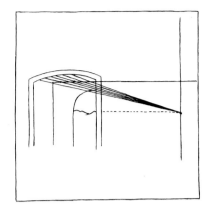

paint them individually by dabbing with a finer brush. I also make intermittent patches of a slightly grey version of the original cream colour in order to reduce the uniformity of colour and make it look more like stone.

As the bottom left-hand corner of the painting contains only massive shapes, I place a brightly coloured rug over one of the horses' backs. In this way I complement the brightness of the scene on the right.

The work is now almost finished. I leave it for a while, then go back and look at it a few times, to see how it can be improved. When I am working on a mural, looking at it the whole time, I get accustomed to what I see and this sometimes blinds me to faults in the painting. For this reason it is a good idea to wait a while – a few days even – then go back and view it with a fresh eye before deciding to varnish.

Far left: *The changing angles of the rafters, parallel in reality, are obtained like this.* Left: *Light and shade on and around the rafters.* Above: *The outside surface of the front arch takes on the appearance of stone.*

CHAPTER FIVE

DIFFERENT TYPES OF TROMPE-L'OEIL AND HOW TO PAINT THEM

Certain kinds of trompe-l'œil *device offer a useful starting point for painting murals. These are largely painted illusions of the most normal everyday things you find in every house: windows, doors and so on. They come in all shapes and sizes, and the artist's imagination can take certain liberties with them which would probably cost an architect his job! For the purpose of demonstration, I have chosen fairly simple examples in the pages which follow.*

I n this chapter we shall look in greater detail at what I call the *trompe-l'œil* elements of mural painting, i.e. those which seem to be part of the architecture and decor of the place in question. We shall assess the value and effect they have in composition, and learn the techniques required to paint them.

WINDOWS

An attractive scene through a window is the most natural and desirable thing, and the painted illusion of an open window is an oft-repeated theme for this reason. There are countless types of window, but for the purpose of demonstration let us take a simple, modern window made of wood and painted white.

Most windows are not flush with the inside wall of a room. They are recessed into the wall. So the first thing to do is to draw the contour of the window recess and the contour of the window frame, plus four connecting lines representing the corners of the recess. If the window is mainly going to be viewed head on, the two sides appear to have the same width.

If the mural is going to be viewed mainly from the left, the window frame contour will appear slightly to the left; if it is going to be viewed mainly from the right, it will appear slightly to the right.

If you want the window recess to narrow down towards the window, you have to take this into account in deciding the angle of the corner lines.

The window frame comes next. This is normally a rectangular wooden frame mounted in the wall. The same angular considerations apply as for the wall recess, i.e. if it is to be viewed mainly from one side, the outside edges appear off-centre.

The illusion of an open window is most effective in creating a sense of three-dimensional space, so now draw in for example one open window and one closed. It is best to draw the window sufficiently open to give a wide view through the open part, but not so wide that you can't also see through the glass.

The position of the open window is decided by its apparent width, and the angles of its upper and lower edges. If the angles are not compatible, the window will not seem square. You sometimes have to play around a bit to get the right angular effects.

As in all realistic painting of this kind, we have to decide which direction the light is coming from, and in a case like this it is a good idea to have the light source – normally the sun, not itself present in the composition – shining against the inside surface of the open window frame. This gives us a direct 'key' to the light source in the painting, which the brain instinctively relates to all other illuminated surfaces beyond, adding a sense of reality to the work. This and any other surfaces of the window facing in the same direction are painted white, which is the lightest colour we have.

One of the problems the artist faces is that in reality we have the colour white – as in the sunlit window frame – and also the light source itself, which may be many times brighter than white.

So the light source itself is best left out of the painting because we have nothing brighter than white to paint it with. However, reflected light can be very effectively used to convey the impression of a bright light source hidden from view.

Once the white parts of the window are painted in, we have to decide which is the next brightest part, and paint it in a warm shade of pale grey, always bearing in mind where the light is coming from and which surfaces would receive more light.

Generally speaking, white surfaces in shade are a warm grey when they are nearby and a cold or bluish-grey when they are more distant. Little by little we paint the window, shading in the darker areas and corners, until we have our completed window.

The painting of the glass itself depends on whether the window is open or closed, and on the angle of the window pane against the line of vision if the window is open.

If the window is closed, we are looking straight through it at right angles – i.e. the angle at which there is naturally least reflection – and in most cases everything outside the window would be much more brightly lit than anything creating a reflection from within the room. Hence there would be no visible reflection. An idea of the presence of glass may in this case be given by painting in a little haze at the corners and along the edges, suggesting areas where the cleaning rag cannot reach.

If the window is wide open, so that the pane of glass is almost parallel with the line of vision, it will reflect almost everything and we can paint a mirror image of whatever would be reflected from that position.

Top row, left to right: *A window recess viewed head on. A window recess viewed slightly from the left. A tapered window recess viewed slightly from the left.* Bottom row, left to right: *The inside contour of the window frame appears off-centre like the inside of the recess when viewed from the left. The scene should still be visible through the glass of the open window. The left-hand window appears rectangular as it should, the right-hand one does not.*

Top: *Creating the illusion of a bright source of light which is not itself in the picture.* Above: *A hazy effect.*

Below: *Various standard shapes of arch.* Right: *The overall dimensions of the arch established at the outset.* Far right: *Drawing the inside surface of the arch.*

The most common case for our purposes, however, and the most difficult, is when the window is partly open, making an angle of about 45° with our line of vision. In this case we can see clearly what is through the glass, and the chances are that we also get some bright light and silhouette reflected off the glass as well.

In order to represent these superimposed images, you should start by painting what is through the glass as if there were no glass there at all, and then draw the outline of whatever is silhouetted against the bright light being reflected – say the outline of a house and some trees. Now, the part of the window surface covered by the reflected house and trees would be darker than what is actually through the glass, so we would see nothing of their reflection – we would just see a clear, normal image of what is through the glass. But the part of the window surface reflecting bright light, for example from the sky close to the sun, would of course be throwing bright reflected light at the eye, and would thus give a hazy, faded look at what lies through the glass in that area. All in all, the whole visible scene through the glass would be divided by the silhouette line into a clear area below, and a hazy area above. This haze I would represent by covering the area in question with a thin, transparent creamy wash, slightly denser perhaps towards the point where the reflected sun would be, i.e. the brightest point.

Exactly the same procedure applies in the painting of other similar structures consisting of glass mounted in wooden frames, such as french windows and doors, except that they are obviously longer, and generally require further *trompe-l'œil* treatment outside in the form of balconies, steps, terraces, etc.

ARCHES

A rugged stone arch in a garden wall, or a moulded one indoors, provides an uncomplicated way of creating a *trompe-l'œil* frame for various kinds of painted composition. The arch has existed as an architectural structure since the earliest times, and comes in various shapes which are widely associated with different cultures and historical epochs.

Here is how to paint a straightforward round stone arch on a garden wall.

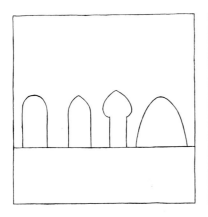

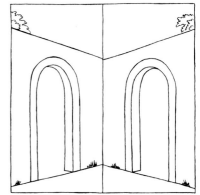

The height of most arches in domestic architecture is about the same as that of the average door, and the width can vary to some extent. In composition this may depend on the size of the area we want to cover, but it should be kept within the bounds of likelihood. The first thing to do is to draw two vertical lines with a semicircular curve at the top to represent the outside contour of the stones. Having decided the width of the stones, draw a concentric line to represent the inside of the arch. These lines give you the geometrical form of the front surface of the arch. You should draw them lightly in pencil, because when you have drawn the stones themselves they will not be required any more. These two contours tell you whether you have got the size and

Part of a large trompe-l'œil *composition containing a formal garden with a regatta and other sporting events, seen through a series of three large french windows. The curtains, windows and wrought-iron balustrade are all in keeping with the existing ones in the house. This dining room also contains blackamoors in painted alcoves and a butler before a mirror.*

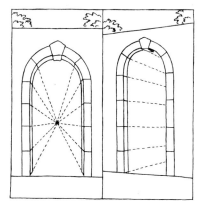

Top: *The perspective rule applies to the joints between the stones.* Centre: *The geometry is now turned into stone.* Bottom: *Stone texture and details of light and shade give substance to the stone.*

shape right. If not, make adjustments at this stage, which saves much time and effort later.

Next, draw another line representing the other side of the arch. As with the window, the main viewing point will decide whether this is concentric or placed to one side or the other. Then draw lines representing the joints between stones on the inside and facing surfaces of the arch. In reality all the lines on the inside of the arch are parallel, so if extended in the drawing they would all meet at the same point on the horizon. The lines on the facing surface of the arch all cut the arch at right angles, hence on the curved part they radiate outwards. I would probably insert a larger keystone at the top, which has a certain decorative effect.

The arch is now complete in its geometrical form, drawn lightly in pencil. Choose the basic stone colour – grey for granite, pale ochre for sandstone, off-white for marble – and paint in the outline of the stones as softer, slightly irregular shapes following the drawn lines. You might deviate from the drawing in places – within the limits of structural plausibility – and paint some of the stones larger or smaller than the others, or cracked and broken. Such details give a feeling of antiquity which can add considerably to the mood of a painting.

When these painted outlines are dry, rub out any bits of drawing that remain outside the limits of the composition. All lines within will be painted over.

You must decide where the light is coming from before you begin painting the arch. This will normally be the main light direction in the place itself, if there is one. Failing that, the choice is arbitrary. If you are painting a well-lit scene beyond, which is normally the case, the inside surface of the arch will be brightly lit on one side, less so on the other, while the curved part above will be the darkest part of the structure. The facing surface will be painted in the normal colour of stone. An important detail in creating the solid appearance of the stones will be the small strips of extended light and shade along the edges of the stones where they join one another.

The texture and colouring of stone varies enormously, and the best way to paint it is to find a suitable example and use its general qualities as a basis for painting. In the case of sandstone for example, one would normally paint the whole facing surface with a light greyish ochre colour – taking care not to lose the joints between the stones – then go over it with a broad, rather dry brush containing a 'dirtier' version of the same. You should use the natural roughness of the surface to help in creating texture, and make sure that this coating is not too monotonous or repetitive. In certain parts you could use the same process with slightly bluish or brown versions of this colour. Use lighter and darker versions of the same to model various dents and kinks in the rough cut surface, since small deviations in vertical surfaces show up more than one would think in terms of light and shade. Towards the bottom you might then add some discreet patches of moss, either of the flat or bulbous variety. The odd tuft of grass growing from a crack can also help.

ALCOVES

The alcove is a useful *trompe-l'œil* device for housing a painted vase, a statue, or some other decorative object. It is best suited to areas already containing the more formal or classical type of decor or garden stonework, and can be effectively used indoors or out. The type and shape of moulding around the outside depends on the style of decor already present, and the shading of the curved inside surface of the alcove depends on the principal light source in the environment in question.

BALCONIES

One important aspect of *trompe-l'œil* mural painting is that of connecting the opening with the scene beyond. In the case of a french window painted in an upstairs room for instance, a very pleasant effect of spaciousness can be achieved by painting a balcony on the other side. It also reinforces the sense of reality our work is to convey.

A painted illusion of a balcony with iron railings is a fairly simple device containing no complex perspective, and you should proceed as follows.

First of all, draw a horizontal line representing the edge of the balcony. The height of the line above the bottom of the painting decides the width of the balcony, and you should place it to give the illusion of a balcony a metre or so (3-4ft) deep. Then draw a pair of horizontal parallel lines to represent the upper railing, and two vertical lines rising slightly above the railing, with perhaps a small urn or *fleur-de-lys* on top. This is the support pillar which will have lighter uprights on either side of it. Also draw another horizontal near the balcony floor to support the uprights.

Now add the uprights and perhaps, but not necessarily, a certain amount of decorative wrought ironwork between them. If the railings are to be black, do not use black paint, because this comes out far too strong in most compositions. Besides, the shiny black paint of most railings in reality reflects light from almost all directions and thus reduces their blackness. For the facing surface of the railings you should use a darkish grey with a hint of blue or brown in it, depending on the general tonality of the painting.

Above: *Various types of alcove with typical contents.*

Far left: *The height of the horizontal lines gives a correct proportion to the balcony.* Left: *It may be composed with or without the decorative ironwork.* Below: *Certain parts of the inner surfaces are hidden from view depending on the angle from which it is viewed.*

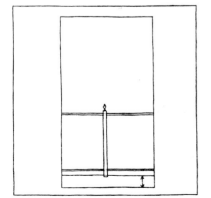
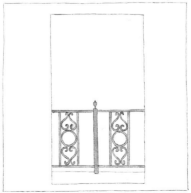

Above: *Shadows, potted plants and a blackbird bring the balcony to life.*

What you have painted so far is the facing side of the various bits of ironwork. Now draw in lightly their inside surfaces, which will be visible at either end of the composition but not in the middle. Depending on the light source, the inside surfaces of the railings will generally be lighter on one side than on the other, since they receive sunlight whereas those on the other side only receive ordinary daylight. Carefully positioned streaks of white on the inside and outside curves of the wrought ironwork will give the impression of bright light on shiny paintwork. Note that when painting a curved surface viewed obliquely, a wrought-iron hoop for example, there will be two points where the inside surfaces disappear completely, because the surfaces coincide with our line of vision, and two points where these surfaces are at their apparent widest, because at these points they are making the widest possible angle with our line of vision. Look at some wrought ironwork from different angles for this effect.

The surface of the balcony can be painted in a warm pale grey as concrete slabs, with one or two joints giving a sense of perspective. The idea of strong sunlight can then be powerfully conveyed by the shadows of the railings falling across the balcony surface. These are painted in a darker, slightly colder grey. The illusion can then of course be completed by the addition of potted plants or other items normally found on balconies.

Trompe-l'œil *at the end of the hall. The curved architrave of the french window repeats a simple pattern existing on other windows and doors. The theme of oriental bridges and philosophers standing in a landscape is the same as that of the bathroom mural shown on pages 34 and 35.*

Opposite: *A flight of ancient stone steps takes the architectural illusion beyond the surface of the wall, and forms a suitable introduction to the landscape beyond.*

Below: *A dreamy English landscape with a lake and bridge. Note the different greens and other colours used in painting the trees. It is important to try and create a 'sense of space', and introduce a bit of action. Down at the lake a dog barks at a jumping fish.*

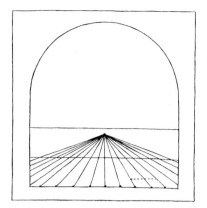 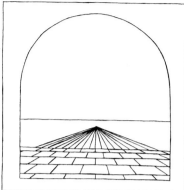 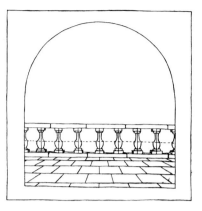

Above: *The perspective lines are drawn half the width of the stones themselves.* Right: *Paving stones drawn in perspective give a strong sense of space.* Far right: *The balustrade is drawn in profile first, then the side surfaces of the support blocks are added using the same perspective.*

TERRACES

In the case of vistas painted at ground level, an appropriate feeling of spaciousness can be achieved by the addition of a wider stone terrace bounded by a stone balustrade.

Here again, start by delineating the far edge of the terrace and the upper surface of the balustrade with horizontal straight lines drawn lightly in pencil. Then decide at what height the horizon would be in reality and mark a vanishing point in the middle. From this point draw a vertical line down to the bottom of the painting area, followed by a series of equally spaced lines radiating downwards from the vanishing point, so that the spaces between them would be half the width of the desired paving stones.

Next, draw a series of horizontal lines below the balustrade which get progressively further apart, and rub out every other section of each radiating line. This gives the positions of a series of staggered paving stones across the terrace.

Now draw in the stone surface of the balustrade, and beneath it so many vertical lines to get the spacing right. Many forms of stone pillar are used in balustrades, but you might choose a typical urn-shaped one to start with. Then draw in the outlines of the pillars as if all were being viewed head on. At either extremity we can see the side surfaces of the mounting blocks above and below the pillars, and in drawing these you should bear in mind the paving stones themselves, because all have a common vanishing point. *Remember*: all parallel lines receding into the picture converge to a single point on the horizon.

The same system of blunting the edges is used here as in the case of the stone arch above. There is no need for the stones to be perfectly regular, and we can make variations within the perspective framework thus created. This illusion of paving stones in perspective is very useful in producing a sense of distance.

In painting the stones themselves we have to bear in mind that this time they are facing upwards and the majority of them will be uniformly lit. Areas of soft shade would occur beneath the balustrade or nearby trees, and hard shadows from the same sources if we are painting a sunlit scene.

Having painted in the basic stone colour and varied it with darker tones in places, you could add various vague areas on separate stones in a pale grey blue, light ochre and a pinkish stone colour, plus one or two more clearly defined areas in a brighter green and orange, to represent surface moss and lichen. If these colourings are done carefully in a balanced way, they give the stonework an attractive iridescent quality without losing the quality of the stone.

Here too it is important to paint shadow on the facing edges of the stones, and thin strips of light on the edges facing the light source. These can either be painted softly to give the idea of curved, worn stones, or as the hard edges of more modern stones. Blades of grass, wild flowers, and the thick, velvety kind of moss can also be placed here and there among the stones.

Next paint the balustrade. This you would normally do as white marble or in the same colour as the paving stones themselves. The upper surfaces receive the most light, and overhanging parts the least. The remainder are painted in intermediate tones. The distribution of light on the pillar itself is slightly more complex, thus best illustrated by a drawing.

Note that the main light source is on the upper left-hand side, thus areas facing upwards on the left are the brightest. Those on the lower right are the darkest. But there is also some light coming from the other side – generally referred to as back light – so a lesser degree of brightness is painted on that side. This means that the most shaded part is slightly to the right of centre. The inset diagram will help to illustrate the phenomenon. It represents a sphere receiving light from one side, and also having reflected light bounced back on to it from the other side.

Above: *The main light falls on one side of the pillar, back light on the other.*

Below: *Here the vanishing point is up in the air, because the parallel lines point upwards.* Bottom: *Note how the upper surfaces of the steps disappear and how the pillars are superimposed on one another.*

STEPS

If the mural is fairly wide, a balustrade right across the middle ground could be rather oppressive, so a flight of stone steps leading up or down to further landscape offers a good solution. Steps are also an ideal introduction to a scene, since more than any other architectural illusion they 'invite' the viewer to go up or down them.

Steps can be placed in a number of ways: in the centre of the balustrade, or on one side or the other, leading away from the viewer towards the horizon, or leading out of the picture sideways to left or right, or both, upwards or downwards.

A robust stone column is placed at the corner of the steps, surmounted by a suitable ornament – usually a sphere, a pineapple or an urn. The balustrade is then continued up or down the side of the steps, and care must be taken in placing the pillars, which are now at different levels and, if the steps are receding, appear to get slightly smaller and closer together as they get further away.

Start by drawing three lines for the upper stones of the balustrade and two lines for its base, all of which culminate in an identical column at the top. This time the vanishing point is up in the air since all the parallel lines are pointing upwards.

Finally, draw so many vertical lines in between to position the pillars themselves.

At the near end we can probably see between the pillars, but as they get further away they are gradually superimposed on one another so that we can only see their right-hand profiles. The upper surfaces of the steps themselves are subject to the law of perspective, so the ones at the bottom will be visible, as if sloping upwards towards a vanishing point, while the surfaces of the upper steps will be hidden by their front edges, as if they were sloping downwards towards the vanishing point. Use an artificial line to position the corners of the steps before you start to draw them, and finally, create the form and texture of the stones in the same way as for the other stone surfaces described above.

COLUMNS

One of the most elegant and suggestive features in architecture has always been the classical stone column. Depending on the type of environment in question, the illusion of such columns incorporated into the wall as supports of the opening itself, or supporting a porch or loggia beyond it, can provide the work with a sense of antiquity and grandeur. A simple form of colonnade for a wide painting might consist of columns built into the wall at either end and one in the middle.

There are three basic types of capital: the Doric, the Ionic and the Corinthian, and the columns themselves normally consist of plain or fluted cylindrical stones mounted one on top of the other.

To create the illusion of a column, start by drawing two vertical lines representing the width of the column. Then draw a square base with perhaps a stone ring on top of it. Now draw another ring at the top of the column, surmounted by an inverted cone section with another square block on top of that. Note the perspective relationship between the blocks and rings at the top and bottom of the column.

The Corinthian is the most elaborate column, having acanthus leaves with corner scrolls above them, hence the most difficult to draw. But it is sumptuous and effective-looking.

The brightest part of the column is of course the edge facing the light source. This light diminishes gradually away from the edge and reaches its darkest point about two thirds of the way round the column, then increases slightly on the other edge.

Below: *Three types of classical column: 1 Doric, 2 Ionic, 3 Corinthian.* Right: *The rough profile and proportion of a classical column.* Far right: *A Corinthian capital has great dignity and decorative appeal.*

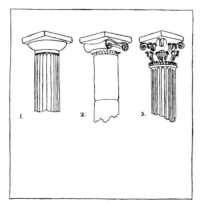

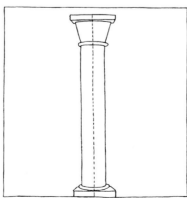

CURTAINS

Curtains and drapes of various kinds are a basic ingredient of mural paintings, and it is important to know how to paint them. Apart from the fact that they are a part of everyday life, to me they have a double symbolic value in painting. Firstly, the presence of cloth in large quantities was always a sign of richness and opulence, especially in ancient times, hence it will generally give this desirable flavour to a painting. Secondly, cloth has always been a means of concealing and revealing things – a most important point. To take the obvious example, the figure of a beautiful woman emerging from behind a curtain is bound to be more curious and exciting than the same figure in full exposure! Another very important function of cloth in painting is that it can be used to portray the wind. A slight variation in its hanging folds, and we have a slight breeze – the kind of detail which truly brings a work to life.

An open curtain is basically a series of hanging tubular folds bunched together, more tightly at the top than at the bottom. You should normally start by drawing the two outermost contours of the curtain from the top of the window to a point just below the windowsill or to the floor, whichever the case may be. Within these limits then draw the divisions between the folds where they actually touch each other forming a cleavage, and leave wider spaces where the curtain just curves inwards without forming a complete fold. These changes in the shape of the curtain should be distributed so as to create an interesting form rather than a monotonous series of tubular shapes.

Towards the edge of the curtain exposed to the open window you can bring the contours out into a gentle curve to give the idea of a piece of cloth being filled with wind. Unless we are painting a storm scene, there is no need to exaggerate this effect. If the curtain is made of a light fabric, the edges affected by the wind may flutter a bit, an effect achieved by creating smaller and more irregular undulations in the cloth.

Any edges of the curtain facing the light from our painted window are the brightest lit. The next brightest are the areas of the folds facing outwards, and the cloth gets progressively darker as it disappears into the folds.

You should generally try to choose a fairly simple fabric design for curtains, because painting a complex design on folding cloth

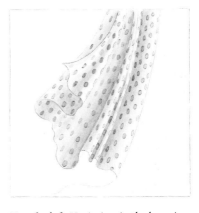

Top, far left: *Variation in the hanging folds of a curtain.* Top left: *The wind made visible.* Top right: *Light distribution on a curtain.* Above: *The changing appearance of poker dots on folding cloth.*

is an extremely arduous and time-consuming task. In this case I have chosen the simplest of all – white curtains with polka dots. The dots on facing areas are round. They are also the brightest in colour as they are in the brightest places. As the cloth recedes into the folds, the dots become progressively more oval in shape as we are not seeing them straight on. They also get darker as the light reaching them is reduced.

In this way we create the illusion of a patterned fabric hanging in folds beside a painted window, and moving in a light breeze. The presence of fabrics of this kind in a mural painting contributes greatly to its integration in the surroundings.

AWNINGS

A cheerful, festive effect can be obtained without great difficulty by incorporating an awning into our work. The advantages of the awning are that, unlike much masonry and woodwork, it can be painted in bright colours, and its structure in painted illusion gives us a powerful sense of three-dimensional space.

In painting murals I am a great believer in the idea of 'space within a space' – in which the space bounded by, for example, a canvas awning and its supporting poles acts as a sort of spatial introduction to the world outside. I use it quite a lot. This spatial introduction may equally be offered by a painted illusion of a conservatory, a porch with columns, a loggia, or even a zone bounded by hedges, an arbour or trees.

In one of my larger works I painted a blue and white striped canvas awning beyond the illusion of a pair of glass doors. Beneath it was a red carpet and beyond it a terrace looking over a fantastic valley. The result of this combination was the kind of festive, romantic mood I wanted.

To paint a simple awning, I start again with pencil lines, marking in the length, width and height I want, two verticals at the far end for each of the supporting poles, three crossbars round the edges of the awning, a triangular structure at the far end, and a bar running along the top. Here too the perspective rule applies, as for all parallel lines receding into the picture, and we have to choose a vanishing point near the horizon.

I then draw in the stripes of the awning, which get progressively wider as they get closer, and curve slightly to give

Below: *The law of perspective applies to the framework of an awning.* Right: *Striped canvas creates an atmosphere of recreation and festivity.*
Far right: *Light passes through the canvas on a breezy day.*

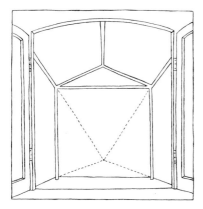
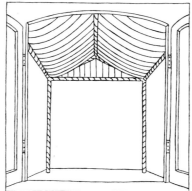
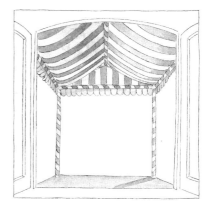

the impression of the weight of cloth. Note that when cloth hangs in this way it is almost straight at the top, the curvature increasing towards the outside. I also wind strips of cloth round the poles in a spiral pattern.

This time we are not dealing with light reflected off a surface – I have to give the impression of light passing through the cloth in the area most directly exposed to the chosen light source in the painting. As the curvature of the cloth changes gradually, the amount of light passing through it changes accordingly, and I have to be careful in gradating my colours in order to achieve this effect. Finally, I include a fringe round the edge, which can be striped like the awning itself, or a different yet compatible colour, such as a gold fringe with a blue and white awning. It can be a single strip of cloth with a wavy or serrated edge, or perhaps a series of loose tongues of fabric hanging separately. The fringe offers the chance to bring some breeze into the painting, and I draw it waving slightly in the moving air.

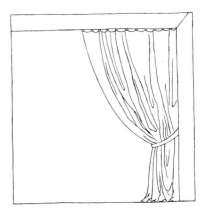

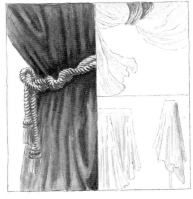

Top: *A large drape forms an imposing frame for a composition.* Above: *Opulence in a twisted golden cord. Hanging drapes can be incorporated in the work in many ways.*

DRAPES

The use of illusions representing draped fabrics can have high decorative value and add considerably to the atmosphere and mystique of a mural painting.

On occasions I have used hanging drapes, suspended bundles of cloth and billowing expanses of fabric as a *trompe-l'œil* frame for my works instead of the usual solid, architectural shapes. This solution can be quite appropriate in irregularly shaped areas that will not accommodate a formal structure. Take a kind of stage curtain for example.

To paint this, first draw the curved outer contour running down from the top to the point where the drape is tied back. Then draw the outer contour of the lower part reaching down to the floor. Note that as with the awning the curved line is straighter at the top than when it approaches its lower support. Next draw lines representing the folds within the fabric itself, which generally follow the shape of the outer contour and get closer to one another near the bottom. The upper edge of the drape can be attached to the ceiling in a series of shallow loops.

There are certain areas where these folds lose their regular hanging shape, because there may be too much cloth bunched together, and form V-shaped creases. These shapes are common in fabric and thus worth studying.

In a case like this you should adopt an interior light source and paint the lights and shades on the fabric accordingly. The tie may well be a heavy golden cord with large tassles at the end and a knot in it. If you feel extravagant you might paint a twisted double cord – far more than would be required to hold back the drape – but this kind of over-abundance can be a most stimulating presence in a painting.

73

CHAPTER SIX

THE WORLD BEYOND THE WALL

Some element of landscape has entered most of the works I have done. I shall now therefore discuss the construction of landscapes, their components, how to create distance, atmosphere and interest in the outside world and the question of fitting them into their respective trompe-l'œil *frames.*

Having created your *trompe-l'œil* illusion, which is like a sort of magical gateway to another world, you have to decide what to put there, because that is really the main part of the painting.

HORIZON

The first thing you should do in creating an imaginary landscape is to decide on the horizon. The distribution of terrain in the distance is closely related to what happens in the foreground, so make a horizon line and put in some tentative lines to represent features in the middle distance. The far distance can normally consist of mountains, ridges, plateaux, rolling hills, plains, towns, lakes and sea. Each of these is represented in simple line drawing in the following sketch.

What you draw on the horizon is entirely a matter of taste, but on the whole flat or flattish horizons are a bit dull and tend to cut the picture in half. You should aim for a balanced mixture of high and low ground, and try to make it surprising and interesting without resorting to exaggeration.

The sight of distant mountains makes us dream – there's no secret about that. Valleys and plains are suggestive of culture, fertility and the active life. Draw them accordingly: the mountains high, wild and remote, with occasional vegetation; the valley or plain containing many hints of life and cultivation.

The power of the brush is much greater when painting details in the far distance. We have to be careful. One little stroke of paint can be a building or a road or hedgerow. Colours are much paler in the distance and normally tend towards blue. But it is very easy to overdo the blueness of horizons, so try to incorporate some pale greys, greens, pinks and ochres to create an acceptable balance.

MIDDLE DISTANCE

The middle distance is lower and generally flatter than the horizon. The colours are stronger and more varied, and the features of the landscape are rendered in greater detail. You would enliven this part of the painting with such things as towns, roads, isolated buildings, lakes, rivers and geological formations.

Right: The horizon and far distance go in first, with lines to indicate middle distance contours. Far right: Topography and detail in the middle distance are suggested by a few brush strokes.

Far left: *A country road enhances the landscape with a sense of movement.*
Left: *Shaded areas on distant water caused by local wind.*

Woods and foliage in general are now close enough for the shapes of individual trees to be seen, but the leaves themselves are not yet discernible.

A town situated on a hill or plain offers a natural focal point for the middle distance. The buildings are still basically seen as blocks of colour, but windows, doors and arches are visible. The town may well be dominated by a church spire, a dome or a tower. Light and shadow are important in giving substance to the form of the town.

Quite often when composing a scene of this kind, even without buildings, one can work away at it but seem to be getting a rather nondescript result. Then you do something, almost unconsciously perhaps, and instead of being just a collection of buildings or trees and fields it suddenly becomes 'a place'. Something in what you see before you sets off a spark of recognition, and you can imagine yourself there. When this happens, you will generally know you have got the composition more or less right.

A country road crossing a hill or flat terrain offers a sense of movement in a still landscape. Roads and dirt tracks often appear lighter in colour than the surrounding terrain, though darker at the edges where grass and foliage create shadow. They may well have a grass ridge down the centre. Trees and buildings are often situated beside roads. Note that when a road, or anything similar in form such as a river, curves in our field of vision, it appears widest at points where it is coming straight towards us, and thinnest when it is running across our field of vision.

The sight of still water conveys a sense of peace and tranquillity. The calm, shiny surface with its muted reflections offers a pleasant counterpart to the endless variations of the landscape around it. Each complements the other.

A distant lake would appear basically as a white strip in the landscape, bounded by the contours of the land on the near side, and by one or more horizontal straight lines representing the shoreline and promontories on the far side. Reflections on distant flat water are often muted and unclear. They may well be broken by horizontal strips of white caused by local gusts of wind disturbing the surface. The shore on the far side is normally bordered by rocks, shrubbery and trees, giving rise to shaded areas which are reflected by a darker fringe on the water beneath them. This again can be broken by strips of white.

There is not a lot of scope for introducing colour into distant water. If the sky is a deep blue, or the sunset very red, or in the presence of dark clouds, some delicately toned strips of colour may be introduced without the water ceasing to look wet!

The surface texture and colouring of still water in the foreground of a painting is more varied and detailed. The darker surface streaks contain something of the colour beneath them, and may be toned in subdued shades of blue, grey-green, brown and maroon. We begin to see the actual ripples on the water, represented by wavy or serrated lines. Still closer to the shore we see the individual ripples which gradually take on the colour of the ground beneath them, and the closer we get the less sky light is reflected to the eye, the more suffused light emerges from the depths. A shiny surface viewed obliquely reflects light far more completely than a shiny surface viewed head on.

Flowing water is a symbol of fertility and plenty. Its presence in a landscape is always a point of reference and a source of interest. Our main endeavour in painting a river must be to give the impression of movement. This is done by depicting irregularities in the surface reflections caused by the flow of water. In the case of a distant river, this can only be done in general terms. Again the water is mainly white, with blue-grey reflections. If the river is in the foreground, we have greater scope for showing a variety of movement and the different colours thrown up by reflections and by the river itself.

The best way to get water moving is of course over a waterfall. Falling water is basically painted white against the darkness of wet rocks. At its uppermost point, where it flows over the edge, we have a shiny curve. But this immediately splits up into various disintegrating columns and frothy masses which get bigger and become less distinct as they descend. The water possibly hits a protruding rock on the way down, which throws it out in a parabolic curve. Again there is froth where the water meets the river surface, as well as a certain amount of fine mist. This is the point of greatest agitation, and we mark it with a churning mass of white. Around it we have a more or less uniform layer of bubbles, which in turn are channelled away by the various currents and gradually disappear.

Represent the movement of falling water by various groups of elongated globules and dotted lines. The parabolic curves of

Right: Surface movement on nearby water. Far right: Try to create a sense of running water.

Above: *If you can hear the water, it's well painted!*

rebounding water have motion written into their shape, because this is the kind of curve made by any thrown object under the force of gravity – a ball for instance. For the shaded parts of water use a pale green with a hint of brown in places where light may be shining through the water, and a mixture of greyish-green and blue-brown tones in places which have less light. Close-up water is hardly ever blue.

The terrain in the middle distance is normally flatter than in the far distance, simply because we don't want it to blot out the horizon. The texture of grass and individual leaves cannot be represented because they are too small to be seen at such a distance. We therefore have to depend on masses of colour to represent fields, hills, etc, and areas of vegetation. Light and shade play an important part as always, and the shadows of individual trees help us to give mood and character to the scene. Fields are normally painted in various greens, often broken up by areas of earth or dry grass, which come out as pale pinks, browny purples and ochres in the distance. Ploughed fields and ripe cornfields dotted across the green landscape give chromatic variety, and what with the bluish elements in shade here and there we have used virtually the whole range of the palette in just creating our middle-distance terrain. It is a good thing to keep the work colourful like this, but care must be taken not to overdo it. What we want is a subtle landscape, not a patchwork quilt! We must also bear in mind the distance in choosing the strength of our colours.

Foliage in the middle distance normally takes the form of woods, coppices, isolated trees and hedgerows. All we can see at this distance is masses of foliage grouped together, and we give them form by distributing light and shade on them in one way or another. Generally you should choose the overall colour of a given group of foliage and paint the whole area in a pale, slightly warm version of that colour, then darken down the areas not receiving direct light. These areas would be cooler in colour, but try to avoid letting them dominate the whole structure. A stippled effect suggesting different degrees of shade will see to this. Not all trees are green, and certain parts of green trees can be enlivened with areas of yellow, brown or red, suggesting dead or dying foliage. Such foliage in shaded areas takes on a purple or maroon appearance in the middle distance. It is a good idea to have some warm hues in areas of shade, otherwise we get so much blue and grey that it becomes monotonous and cold. Certain parts of the illuminated foliage can be heightened with stronger pinks and yellows, or pale, yellowish greens, but these should not be overdone or the areas in question will lose the effect of light.

Tree trunks and branches in the middle distance generally appear blue or browny purple against a lighter background. If they are on the edge of a dense wood, they will appear lighter against the darkness beyond.

Among the green trees you could place some red, brown blue and ochre ones, but care must be taken not to make these colours too bright or they will look unreal and the group of trees will lose its homogeneity. The same process of shading applies as for green trees.

Trees must have character. They must look as if they are growing. Try to incorporate a sense of movement or rhythm in the developing curves and angles of their trunks and branches. In one of my early works I painted a pair of tall trees standing out above the others which appeared to be dancing – I could have sworn they were in love!

FOREGROUND

Having already dealt with certain structural components which can be placed in the immediate foreground – terraces, etc. – we must now consider what to do immediately beyond them.

Quite possibly there would be some kind of gravel forecourt or driveway immediately beyond our *trompe-l'œil* structure, and this in turn might be surrounded by rough-cut grass or lawns. You should not attempt to paint a thick layer of homogeneous gravel in such an area. Apart from the difficulty of execution, I believe it would look too artificial. Far more interesting and appropriate is a beaten earth surface with stones and pebbles strewn across it in an irregular manner, to give the impression of a transit surface that has been worn flat with use over the years.

To create this illusion you should first of all cover the entire area with a suitable pale earth colour, which may be a warm grey, an ochre, or a light terracotta. Then vary it in places with other similar earth hues, darken it gradually towards the edge away from the light source in order to give the idea of a cambered surface, and paint in any hard shadows cast by trees, etc. Shadows here should be painted in a darker version of the earth colour in question, perhaps leaning very slightly towards blue or purple, but not too much. Another important feature is the narrow strip of shadow along the edge of the driveway which is caused by the grass verge. Border shadows of this kind play an important part in giving substance and definition to flat painted areas. Last of all, distribute your pebbles, some in the form of thin rows of coloured dots and dashes strewn across the driveway, representing smaller grit and pebbles, others in groups of two or three larger pebbles, casting individual shadows.

Lawns on the whole should not be too well kept. A perfectly mown, perfectly flat lawn, with those proverbial stripes where the mower has been, can be rather a boring sight. Certainly start with a flat pale green colour when painting lawns, but then add some interest in the form of numerous little ridges of darker colour where the grass has grown, maybe one or two patches of almost bare earth, and some ochre-coloured dry grass. There is no need to paint actual blades of grass all over the lawn, especially in the distance. In the very close foreground there obviously has to be a higher density of grass texture to flat colour. If an area appears too flat, take a well-used 3cm (1 in) decorator's brush with uneven bristles and execute a series of light vertical strokes in a colour slightly darker than the green in question. If the lawn comes up against a pillar or wall – places where the

Below: *Detail and variety on a stony path.*

mower cannot reach – also insert some larger tufts of grass in a darker colour.

Rough grass on uneven terrain is often required in mural painting. Here there is greater scope for playing with light and shade. There is a wider variety of colours present in unkempt grass: pale ochres, browns, yellows and a higher percentage of pinks than one would imagine. Clusters of poppies, daisies, buttercups etc. in brighter colours add the finishing touch which turns a patch of rough grass into a vital, iridescent part of our painting. Much can also be done by the way we bend the long grass in the foreground to give an impression of wind and a lively sense of movement.

A large tree in the foreground or a group of trees a little further away can serve the useful purpose of providing a centre of gravity in the composition. This is important. What you might call the 'tension' between the bulk of a large tree or group of trees, and the empty spaces around and beyond them, can be one of the vital forces in a painting. Depending on the way they are composed, the presence of trees can also give us that 'space within a space' which you can aim to have in your paintings.

In painting a tree closer to the beholder, we have to consider not only the various masses of foliage of which it is composed, but also the leaves themselves, because now they are visible. You should start by drawing a rough outline of the various masses of foliage, to give the tree the overall shape you want, then decide where the branches would have to be in order to support that foliage. After drawing in the trunk and branches, start to put in more detailed outlines showing the leaves themselves. Gradually add more profiles of leafy clusters within these outlines, to give the impression of a large number of leaves superimposed on one another. The outer profile of the tree itself must not be too clear-cut. There are always a few leaves sticking out beyond the others, and their presence in the composition is important to give that necessary feeling of random growth.

In painting the foliage, start with the parts exposed directly to light. These you should paint in a pale, yellowish green, adding tints of cooler and warmer yellows here and there. If we confine our tree to one colour it will be monotonous, but if the variety of hues is too wide we shall lose the desired effect. All parts not exposed to direct light are then painted in a darker green, ochre

Right: *Close-cropped and long grass occur frequently in natural compositions.* Far right: *A large tree and its shadow can create an enclosed atmosphere to offset the open landscape.*

and reddish tinges being added here and there, especially towards the ends of branches. Then add the darker hues of parts in deeper shade, making sure you avoid blocks of hard-edged colour by introducing leafy forms at the edges.

Tree trunks normally have a cracked grain running along them, or rings going round them, depending on the type. Some, such as plane trees, have large areas of differentiated colour which resemble camouflage. Light and back light are important in giving form and substance to the trunk and branches, and a certain amount of root should be visible above the ground.

In order to avoid having all the interest at ground level and nothing but blue sky and clouds at the top of our opening, some

One for the loo! Painted in half an hour, this porthole window shows how a more spontaneous, impressionistic style can be used to paint a trompe-l'œil *in the right surroundings.*

Above: *Greater detail is evident in nearby foliage.* Right: *Rockery and shrubs provide a refreshing break in a panoramic scene.* Far right: *The artist can indulge his fantasy as the noble lord once did.*

spreading fronds or blossoms can effectively be brought into the upper edges of the picture as if from trees or climbers hidden from view on either side. These are so close that the individual leaves must now be painted in greater detail. Various large-leafed species, perhaps with brightly coloured flowers, can also be located against the lower part of the structure to complete a kind of secondary 'verdant' frame of our work.

The presence of rocky outcrops or groups of large boulders in the foreground and middle distance of our composition can give it a touch of wildness and romance, or at least of the proximity of untamed nature. As with the waterfall, stunted trees and flowering shrubs can appropriately be set against a rocky background. The oriental painters were fond of such combinations. I often choose to include the stratified, sedimentary type of rocks in my paintings, because the history of their geological formation can be seen in the various layers of stone.

Men designing landscapes and planning gardens have often felt the need to incorporate buildings in their creations. Whether it be a pavilion or gazebo, or some kind of folly, or just a potting shed or outhouse at the end of the backyard, more often than not they sign their presence by some permanent kind of structure. So in painting, the carefully situated presence of a decorative or utilitarian building can be highly complementary to the surrounding landscape. Quite simply, if we place a small temple or a pavilion or pagoda in the painting, not only is it a decorative object in its own right, but we can also imagine being there and enjoying the same landscape from a different point of view. This kind of feature plays a big part in creating a 'sense of place' in the work, which helps to give it character and bring it to life.

Another kind of structure which is always a most agreeable presence in a painted landscape is the bridge over still or running water. The painted reflection of a bridge is one of the best ways of painting still water, especially if the view beneath it dissolves in mist and light or leads to a distant shoreline.

The blue of a blue sky is at its deepest overhead, and gradually gets paler towards the horizon. On a very clear day, and generally in drier climates, this change is not great. The deeper blue reaches almost down to the horizon. In misty, humid climates however, it can almost change from blue overhead to white or a very pale blue on the horizon.

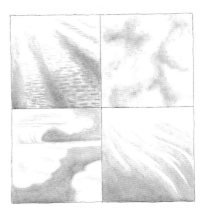

The type of cerulean blue widely available in different brands – from the Latin word *caelum* meaning the sky – is in my opinion too strong and cold to be used alone in painting sky, even when mixed with white. It has a sort of turquoise harshness about it. Ultramarine is a darker, warmer blue. A mixture of this with a smaller amount of cerulean and plenty of white – a top quality commercial brilliant-white matt emulsion will do – is about as close as one can get to the true blue. Of course, the particular colour we choose depends to a large extent on taste, and also on the mood and coloration of the picture. Certain artists have favoured a harder, colder blue, but in painting natural scenes I think there is always a danger of making the whole thing too cold, what with all those greens and blues. The French artist Boucher is reputed to have said: 'the trouble with nature is that it is too green and badly lit!' So a lot can be done to avoid this possible imbalance by a careful choice of sky blue. On certain occasions I have even added a hint of purple, to match a large expanse of sky in an indoor painting with a particular colour scheme.

Clouds come in various forms, and contain various degrees of shade. The most dreamy and romantic are cirrus clouds, those high wispy ones often seen in isolation against a clear sky. The shape of such clouds can give rise to all kinds of emotion, and the presence of one or two of them can make all the difference in what might otherwise be rather an empty, monotonous blue sky.

Nimbus, those large, bulbous, solid-looking clouds, usually with white edges and grey undersides, can create a strong impression etched against a blue sky, but we have to be careful not to make them look too hard and regular in shape. The sky can also be broken up with areas of soft, mottled cloud without hard edges, which give a vapourish tone to the painting. A finer version of this type is the mackerel sky, especially effective when painted in wedge-shaped strips above a red sunset.

In painting all these clouds you should start by doing a clear sky, then make an outline of the cloud area, not in white but in a slightly lighter version of the sky blue. You should then fill the areas in question with a yet lighter blue and gradually take it towards white in its densest parts. Shading would then be added where required, normally in a soft purplish grey colour, again gradating the colour to avoid hard edges. This process of creating

Far left: A bridge over still or running water as a decorative point of reference in a rural scene. Left: A landscape exploding with life. Above: Different cloud forms can vary the mood of a painting quite a lot.

soft-edged clouds can be applied in varying degrees, depending on the softness required, or hardly at all if the desired effect is that of hard-edged clouds.

The greater the contrast between light and shade in a cloud, the more likely we are to have a storm! Storm clouds are a useful tool in creating dramatic effect and a sense of apprehension in a painting. I have recently used them in a painting of the Crucifixion above the altar of an Italian chapel.

In the case of a sunset, the edges of clouds receiving light can be tinged with pink and gold, but this must be done lightly because strong colours – especially reds – appear darker and lose the effect of light.

One of the ways of making distant landscape appear far away is by adding mist. To do this when working in acrylics, take a little white paint in a lot of water, well mixed, and brush it lightly all over the distant parts with a 3cm (1 in) decorator's brush; then while it is still quite wet rub it over carefully with a dry cloth. The white paint should be very watery, and if the effect is not strong enough, you can always go over it again. In the case of high mountains in the distance, a good effect can be created with streaks of a slightly stronger white – still soft and indistinct – passing across the steep surfaces, to give an atmospheric feeling of layered mist.

One of the most beautiful phenomena in all of nature is the range of colours in a sunset sky. According to my observations, the changing spectrum is as follows: deep blue, light blue, pale green, white, yellow, orange, red, purple, grey. These colours should be blended into one another very carefully, and in many cases all that is required to give an idea of sunset, or sunrise, is a pale blue blending down to yellow. Cadmium reds and yellows are very strong colours, but also very hard and rather unnatural. They can be mixed sparingly with ochre and red earth, plus lots of white, to obtain a good blend of colours for a sunset sky.

URBAN SCENE

If buildings are to be the main feature in the foreground and middle distance of our composition, the first thing we have to do is to try and achieve an interesting layout, a 'sense of place', so to speak. One way of doing this is to locate the buildings at different

Right: *An irregular layout gives character to the town.* Far right: *A slight departure from naturalism can yield a harmonious, restful composition.*

angles in our field of vision. I would normally start by sketching out the various buildings in rough, then establish the likely vanishing points in question, and draw in the various parallel lines accurately according to the normal system of perspective.

A suitable combination of facing surfaces of buildings and receding planes can give a certain dynamic quality to the work, as for example in the far side of a square and the various fronts of buildings receding at different angles down a long street.

The fronts of buildings can be in different styles with different kinds of architectural features, and the square in the foreground offers the chance to introduce some livelier colour and 'real' movement into the picture. Figures, awnings and a public garden for instance will see to this. It is also hard to resist the insertion of a bit of landscape in the far distance.

SURREALISTIC SCENE

A combination of real things outside their normal places in nature, or painted in an idealized setting, can make an extremely decorative subject beyond the *trompe-l'œil* divide. Elements of landscape, perspective and distance in such a composition will moreover help to ensure that the value of the *trompe-l'œil* element is not wasted, i.e. that of opening the environment up. Take a classical seascape with an urn and a Grecian figure for example.

Trompe-l'œil operates by virtue of precise visual illusion – the painted imitation of something real and solid. Surrealism is an appeal to the senses and the memory by means of suggestive, at times unlikely, combinations of imagery. You might say that these two disciplines lie at opposite ends of the 'fantasy spectrum'. There are no rules, and in combining the two we are covering unusual ground where anything could happen!

A PATTERNED SCENE

We can even go further away from reality if we wish, and wander towards the world of decorative wallpaper, by marrying re-peated, stylized images with a sense of distance. Oriental blossoms and blackbirds might be a suitable combination for example, on rocks and misty islands.

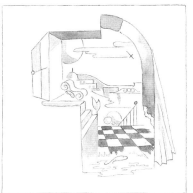

Far left: *Further into the realm of pure decoration.* Left: *Our precious sense of space can be preserved in a composition bordering on abstraction.*

AN ABSTRACT COMPOSITION

Although I have never done it in practice, I can see no reason why an abstract composition might not fit into a *trompe-l'œil* frame, if anyone is inclined to try it.

The art of abstract painting consists of representing forms, or groups of forms, divested of all the details and characteristics – except perhaps for colour – which make them into recognizable things. In a case like this, an extremely simple *trompe-l'œil* frame would probably be best, such as a box opening in the wall with no architectural details and no recognizable materials. In the extreme, even this so-called 'real' part of the painting and its concomitant perspective could be dissected and analysed under the painter's brush.

CHAPTER SEVEN

LIVING FORMS
IN MURAL PAINTING

*Human figures, animals, birds and fish can bring a picture to
life, especially if portrayed in a sensitive, lively or humorous way.
The butler reflected in a painted mirror with the reflection of the
main mural in the background is a case of this. Certain species
tend to be more at home than others in a mural painting, and
they will now be dealt with in their various possible settings.*

Many of the greatest artists throughout the ages have aspired to paint the human figure. Entire lives have been devoted to the effort. But this does not mean that we lesser mortals cannot have a go as well. Every child who ever lifted a pencil instinctively drew a little bundle of lines with blobs for its feet, a circular head, and a grin on its face. So, somewhere deep in our nature we have a desire to draw our own likeness on a flat surface! The fact that most life classes in London night schools seem to be permanently over-subscribed also testifies to this.

Nothing more effectively brings a work of art to life than the presence of a human figure. Of possible human figures there is an infinite number, and each of them can be painted in an infinite number of ways.

THE SOLITARY FIGURE

One figure sitting, standing or walking slowly in a landscape can essentially be a pensive figure or a dreamer. The position and angle of the head is perhaps the clearest indication of the thoughts inside, apart from the facial expression if the figure is close enough for its features to be seen. The position and gesture of hands are also a most important part of creating mood.

In our approach to painting figures we have to bear in mind that they cannot talk – their only means of communication are those of facial expression, gesture, posture, and a sense of movement. In this respect the painted figure is in the same position as the mimic and the dancer in the theatre. Before we start to paint the human figure in action it is a good idea to consider these theatrical figures and how they communicate without words.

For a given position of the body, that of a seated female figure for example, the way we position the head can be a decisive factor in establishing the mood of the figure, and ultimately of the painting. Note that in this case the body is slightly bent in a position of relaxation. This suggests a certain lassitude for a start. The free hand is deliberately resting on the girl's leg, contributing nothing to her expression. Yet each of the four positions of her head alone yields a different mood.

Unless you are painting a scene of stress and exertion, try to keep your bodily poses fluid and relaxed. They must of course be natural, and it is most important to distribute the weight correctly. Artists have been positioning figures in painting and sculpture for two or three thousand years, and you should find traditional ideas about poise and elegance quite acceptable. However, never copy another artist's work, and do not feel you need to use models. You can invent your figures by experimenting with a pencil and paper and an india rubber. Contrary to what many art teachers say, there is nothing in the least shameful about rubbing out! If any anatomical detail presents a problem, you might ask someone to assume a position for a couple of minutes so that you can do a quick sketch. As often as not you can get your visual information by looking at parts of

Below: *1 Wistful, 2 Pensive, 3 Sympathetic, 4 Envious.*

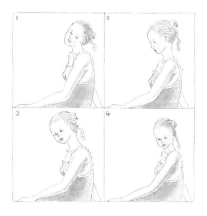

  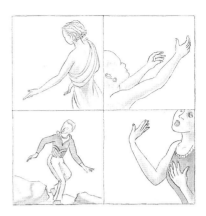

Far left: *A solitary, seated figure with whom we can share a feeling.* Left: *Typical stances for the solitary figure in a landscape.* Above: *The hands are a key to many a situation.*

your own body in the mirror. The necessary adjustments for a figure of the opposite sex can then be made on paper! Unless you are doing a period piece, try to keep your costumes simple and timeless, but more about costumes later.

My standing figures are rarely bolt upright with their hands by their sides. A sense of rhythm has to be introduced into their posture, and I find that some kind of manual gesture – not excessive – helps to give interest and vitality to the static figure. A figure standing at a vantage point gazing into the distance, preferably in the presence of other vertical forms, will have the effect of reinforcing the viewer's own sentiments in looking into the picture.

A standing figure engaged in some form of action, such as taking a flower or fruit from a tree, or even leaning against a flat surface chewing a piece of grass, will start to bring a storyline into the picture and thus give it a whole new dimension of interest. A figure pacing slowly across the landscape at some distance from the viewer will have a similar effect.

MOOD AND EXPRESSION

Like the positioning of the head, the way we place the arms and hands of our figure is an important factor in the creation of mood, especially when the figure is more distant and the facial features are not so easily discernible.

Typical cases where the hands come into play are those of offering, taking, maintaining the balance of an unstable figure, or expressing a stronger emotion such as joy, sorrow, shock or surprise. The eyes and mouth are the two mobile parts of the face, and the way we paint them decides the expression of the face. Obviously we cannot learn to do this overnight – the human face is the most subtle and variable thing in the whole of nature. All the more reason for trying to paint it! But a few basic hints about the variations of the eyes and mouth can set us on the right road towards creating the desired effect. The drawing overleaf shows six expressions of the eye and six of the mouth. For any given eye or mouth there is an endless number of possible expressions, and of combinations of expression between the eye and mouth. Study these expressions for a while, and then try a few of them in the mirror.

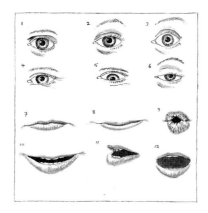

Above: *The eyes and mouth are the most directly expressive part of the human body.*

1 The eye in its normal relaxed state. Note the position of the eyebrow. The iris sits on top of the lower eyelid, and its upper part is hidden by the upper eyelid. There is a small spot of light on the edge of the pupil, and the lighter inside part of the iris, where it surrounds the pupil, is slightly brighter on the side opposite the spot of light.

2 If the eyebrow is raised but the upper eyelid remains in its normal position over the iris, the result is a slightly sad or wistful expression.

3 If the eyebrow is raised and the upper eyelid is also raised so that we see the white of the eye above the iris, we achieve an expression of surprise.

4 If the eyebrow is in its normal position and the flesh below the lower eyelid is bunched up so that its contour meets or covers it, we get a feeling of tenderness or affection. This effect can often be achieved with a single curved line below the eye when painting more distant faces. The effect can be seen on the face of the girl sitting on a rock in the drawing above.

5 If the eyebrow is lowered, the lower eyelid raised to cover almost half of the iris and pupil, and the white of the eye visible above the iris, we get an expression of ferocity.

6 If the eyebrow is raised and the upper eyelid lowered across the iris and pupil, our face will assume an attitude of boredom.

7 The mouth in a state of repose. The only hard line of the mouth when painted on a normal scale is that of the joint between the closed lips. In distant faces the outer contours of the lips sometimes have to be represented by painted lines, because the mouth is too small to accommodate any further detail. The joint between the lips is very variable, and an important key to character and recognition. There is normally a narrow strip of shadow beneath the joint. The upper lip is a little lighter than this in general, and the lower lip varies from shiny reflection to a darker lip tone. The corners of the mouth are another important key to expression, especially when the mouth is not in a position of repose.

8 In a half smile the centre line is drawn outwards and often upwards at the ends, but the upward curve of such a smile should not be exaggerated, unless we want to paint a grinning idiot! The lower lip generally appears thinner and smoother and the strip of shadow beneath the joint gets thinner or disappears.

9 A mouth bunched up in an expression of surprise has thin radial lines around the edges and thick fleshy folds at the centre. The teeth are not visible.

10 The teeth become visible when the smiling mouth is open. In many cases the closed mouth is associated with introversion, meanness and frigidity, the open mouth with extroversion, generosity and sensuality. Of course there can be no rule about this, but it is worth bearing in mind when composing figures.

11 An open mouth viewed from the side. Visible teeth should not be too big or exposed. The upper front teeth are considerably larger than the lower front teeth. The outer contours of the lips should be soft and blurred, unless we want to create an image of heavy lipstick. The corners of open and closed mouths should be kept soft as well. No hard lines in the corners.

12 The 'come-hitherish' look. A mouth drooling and limp with desire!

The above examples of course only scratch the surface of one of the most complex and absorbing subjects in art: the human face. I believe that a lot of peole who could get satisfaction out of painting the human figure in different ways never actually try because they think it is too difficult. What I am doing here is trying to create the enthusiasm for it and persuade them to make a start. There is nothing to lose.

The first of six round panels on mirrored wardrobe doors, depicting a continuous river scene with waterfalls and rapids plus a wide range of real, legendary and extinct species of animals, birds and creatures of the deep.

Above: *Distant figures in rudimentary form can make the difference between an empty setting and a lively scene.*

FIGURES IN COMPANY

Often it is a good idea to place more than one figure in your paintings. If we have two figures in the foreground for instance, the relationship between those two figures becomes the main theme of the painting, whether they are each responding to the presence of the other, or only one of them is aware of the other's presence. There seems little point in painting two figures who are unaware of or unmoved by each other's presence. The mimic or dancer's art comes into play more prominently when there is more than one figure in the painting.

I do not normally paint large groups of figures in the foreground of my paintings. But groups of vestigial figures in the further distance can be an effective presence – not demanding huge amounts of painting effort – to create an atmosphere of life and activity around the centre-piece of the work.

HAIR, COSTUME AND HEAD-DRESS

Ideally the artist should be an expert on everything, but this is impossible, so we just have to come as close as we can. Never more than in our role as couturier and coiffeur! The kinds of hair-do it is easiest to favour are fairly natural and not immediately associated with any epoch. Hence a lady with straight hair gathered into a bun, with or without a hanging tail, is quite appropriate in many situations. It also has the advantage that you can see her neck – always a valuable attribute of the female figure. Long flowing hair can be attractive, but it has to be managed carefully and should not be overdone. Long red hair can be very striking. A short, slightly boyish style can also be an alluring solution. Perhaps in his heart of hearts the artist really wants to find perfect beauty in sexlessness!

Male hair can be done in a dense mass of cropped curls, or combed straight back with a slight wave at the ends. Wild, dishevelled hair can be amusing in the right circumstances. The old man with long grey hair and a beard is also a timeless, oft-repeated presence in painting.

As was said above in respect of hair, unless the work is to have a particular period flavour, you should normally aim to clothe your figures in simple, transcendent clothing not specific to any age or style, but vaguely applicable to different times and places.

Right: *Various types of hairstyle for the female figure.* Far right: *Various types of hairstyle for the male figure.*

Far left: *Garments belonging to no particular epoch enhance the timeless quality of a composition.* Left: *Carnival costumes, legendary figures and formal dress for the festive, romantic mood in a painting.*

For a woman this might be a plain long gown of light fabric with a sash and minimal decoration; for a young man a pair of tight trousers or hose, a loose shirt and a jerkin; for an old man a loose-fitting robe. In most of my works the more typically modern types of outfit would seem to be out of place.

In certain kinds of composition formal dress is quite suitable – morning wear, evening wear, livery – partly because they have a timeless quality about them.

Perhaps my favourite type of costume is that of the *carneval* or *commedia dell'arte* tradition. I have always found Pierrot, Harlequin, Columbine, Pulcinella, etc., to be enchanting, ageless characters, and quite at home in my more festive compositions. The tradition of circus dress has also on occasion offered inspiration for the creation of more fanciful costumes and head-dresses in my less realistic works.

ANIMALS, BIRDS, ETC.

Murals containing natural scenes should nearly always include some forms of animal life. It would be a contradiction to exclude them. From the point of view of composition they are an obliging lot, because they come in all shapes and sizes, all colours, and they can be located on the ground, in the air, up trees, among the flowers, and occasionally even jumping out of the water!

As with humans, we must know something about their anatomy and behaviour before we can start to paint them, and there is no substitute for just sitting down and studying pictures of them or the real thing. One of the great pleasures of painting murals is that we do have to study different things, and so pick up a lot of interesting information which otherwise might never come to our notice. This is the case with animals and birds, and one easy way in which you can learn something about them is to collect a few general zoological books.

The large four-legged species – notably horses, cattle and deer – can be suitably placed in large fields and hillsides in the middle distance, to form a little patch of interest in an open space, either moving or standing still. Two of the classic editions which belong on every artist's shelf are Muybridge's *The Human Figure in Motion* and *Animals in Motion*, both available at a reasonable price from Dover Press.

Below: *Animals moving and standing still create a point of interest in a peaceful landscape.*

When I first entered Robert and Sandi Lacey's bedroom in their new house,
there were floorboards missing and there was no paint on the walls. When I left
it for the last time, it could only be described as 'other Eden, demi-Paradise'!
One of the main features of their concept were the built-in wardrobes – six in all
– with mirrored double doors and a large medallion in the centre of each. My
job was to paint them.

The terms of reference were to paint a series of compositions with real and
legendary birds and beasts, including extinct species. They particularly wanted
a dodo. The remaining surfaces of the room were due to be pearlized in very
pale shades of silky enamel applied with a spray, to give a multicoloured,
dappled effect. My composition therefore had to be similarly pale and delicate in
its coloration, in order to harmonize with the project.

I chose to paint the continuous progress of a river through idealized terrain, starting with a waterfall and a deep pool in the first panel, then passing through a varied, meandering course to culminate in rapids on the panel closest to the Jacuzzi bath at the far end of the bathroom.

The round panels were each about a metre (3ft) in diameter, and a similar structure of composition was used in most of the panels: a small amount of land was visible at the bottom of the painting, in the form of grass, reeds, shrubs, flowers, pebbly shore, etc. – possibly as the support for animals and birds. The river itself took up the bottom third or half of the medallion, and beyond that an area of flat terrain with trees and perhaps low hills would lead to a more mountainous landscape in the distance. This kind of mural contains no trompe-l'œil *at all.*

Right: *Mythical beasts are very much at home in mural painting.* Far right: *Birds are a useful decorative device because they can be placed anywhere.*

Family pets, normally in the shape of cats and dogs, frequently find their way into my paintings. In one household the family cat actually tried to walk down a flight of steps I had done on the wall, and got quite confused. Of course, there could only be one reward for believing my steps were real: immortality. The cat now sits in splendour for all time at the top of that flight of steps.

Mythical beasts – dragons, unicorns, chimeras – can add a touch of magic to a mural. In designing the bodies of such beasts there is more scope for imagination than in painting existing species.

Birds are a must in most paintings. Swans on lakes, peacocks on terraces, a cock on the haystack, or geese in the garden. We can also put smaller birds among the foliage, either flying or perched on the branches. Small birds flying in distant sky are not very effective. Unless the mural is viewed from close up they just look like dark spots in the sky. I sometimes paint brightly-coloured imaginary tropical birds swooping in pairs across the foreground of my paintings. There is plenty of scope for inventing imaginary types of bird.

I always try to make my animals look lively and intelligent. In certain paintings of the older schools the animals almost seem to have human expressions on their faces.

The pathetic fallacy – in which inanimate objects are attributed with human feelings – is common enough as a literary device. Shakespeare used it: 'So I shall tell my troubles to the stones . . .' It is also a perfectly normal part of our everyday way of thought. This natural tendency, to elicit emotional responses from things which are really incapable of making them, can be effectively exploited by the artist as a way of giving more power and interest to his painting – not only in the case of inanimate objects like rock formations and trees, or moving water, but also with regard to animals and birds. Whether the non-human species actually have feelings akin to those of humans may be an academic question, but there is no doubt that humans treat them as though they do. So why not paint them as though they do? The smiling Cheshire Cat in Alice is a prime example of this. I was deeply impressed by a reconstruction which Rubens made from Leonardo da Vinci's drawings for the lost fresco of the Battle of Anghiari, in which the horses' faces present a picture of exquisite wrath in a scene of war. Without any distortion of the true

Far left: What would a fish think if it knew it was being painted? Left: Horses can form a kind of 'moving frieze' on the horizon.

anatomy of the horses' faces, he managed to imbue them with the strongest human feeling.

I also firmly believe in adding the comic touch. Whether it be in the attitude and facial expression of human beings, animals, birds, or even fish, a little humour or tomfoolery can be the very thing which sets the work alight. For quite a long time artists have been taking themselves too seriously. I don't know why it happened, but I think it might have started with all those dreary portraits which the French Impressionists did. They were so absorbed with producing texture, and creating optical effects, that they seemed to forget the faces they were painting actually had real people inside them!

The introduction of non-human species into our painting provides a useful opportunity to include some vigorous motion into a still landscape. As with the juxtaposition of mass and space in a painting, a lively tension can be achieved by the interplay of stillness and motion. A fish jumping from a still pool – possibly with a look of mild surprise on its face – or a team of wild horses racing on a bleak escarpment, will give our work an extra 'storyline' which stimulates the viewer and provides enduring interest. Butterflies, dragonflies, coloured beetles and other real or imaginary small species can then be subtly hidden in nearby foliage or perched on window frames for the further embellishment of the picture.

CHAPTER EIGHT

TROMPE L'OEIL DEVICES ON THIS SIDE OF THE WALL

The main trompe-l'œil *structure is normally painted as part of the wall in the form of some kind of opening. We then have auxiliary structures in the imaginary space beyond the wall — terraces, etc. But the illusion can also be considerably enhanced by various painted components which in reality would be on this side of the wall.*

Certain *trompe-l'œil* effects in shallow perspective can be painted on this side of the wall, either alone or as a complement to a *trompe-l'œil* opening with a scene beyond. Wooden or painted panelling is a typical example of this.

Panelling on walls has a very shallow perspective, and so we cannot rely too much on perspective itself to give the impression of depth. We therefore have to depend largely on light and shadow. As wooden panelling is normally made up of different pieces of wood, we are also helped by the grain of the wood which runs in different directions. We have to decide the shape of the panels in terms of the dimensions of the wall, so that it can be divided up equally into rectangles or squares. This is a job for the calculator, and once the shape is decided we must design the panel. It can, for instance, be a flat rectangle of wood with a fluted moulding around it. We start by drawing the geometrical outline of the entire panel.

We have to decide the light source before we start shading and creating the wooden texture. This is usually dictated by the position of windows in the room, and so would be to one side or the other rather than above. The next thing to do is to choose a colour of wood and cover the whole area with a pale, slightly yellowish version of this colour, except for the edges which would be reflecting light. This would normally involve leaving strips of white along the relevant curved surfaces of the moulding.

Seasoned, treated wood is often a warm light colour inside with darker coatings on the surface. Ideally we want this natural colour to glow through at the finish, a point which must be borne in mind when adding subsequent layers of paint.

At this point, you should take a fine brush and a very slightly darker version of the base colour to paint in the main features of the grain. On the narrow moulding this would take the form of straightish lines, irregularly spaced, whereas on the panel itself you could introduce a knot or two and the various concomitant lines which 'flow' around them. Again the lines of the grain should be irregularly spaced, but not too much so, and varied in width and weight. Most wood also contains strips of darker colour in general, each one consisting of a variable number of grain lines. The grain should be faded out at the edges of the white strips representing reflected light. If the pale lines representing the wood grain seem convincing, they can be strengthened in varying degrees by a darker wood colour to prevent them being lost under subsequent layers of paint.

Now cover the parts of the panel and moulding in shade with a darker, slightly cooler version of your chosen wood colour, going very carefully and avoiding at all costs using colours that are too dark too soon.

This process depends on working carefully from light to dark. If we have to lighten parts which are too dark, the effect will be spoilt by the presence of blue haze. If something gets out of control and we have to cancel out, the best thing to do is to paint white a suitable area bounded by a grain line and do that area again from scratch. This will avoid blotches and tide marks. In

painting the wood colour it is best to use transparent colours containing little white. We can do this by using a thin wash, but care must be taken not to let the paint run across the grain lines. It is best to work with a fairly dry brush. Alternatively we can use an acrylic gel, which gives body to the paint without making the colour too heavy or opaque.

Some of the darkest grain usually occurs around knots among the lines disturbed by their presence. These should now be strengthened carefully. Some may be thicker than others, and the thicker ones may be hard-edged on one side, faded on the other. Now is the time to fill in those darker 'rivers' flowing through the grain. Having filled the heavier grain lines, now take a broader brush with a small amount of darker wood colour on it, and paint in the finer grain by following the coarser lines very lightly, so that not all the bristles are touching the surface. This process may be repeated more than once, always lightly and carefully, to build up the lighter grain.

The overall tone of the wood may be varied by applying deeper, richer, warmer or darker areas here and there, always bearing in mind the direction of grain. At this stage the areas in deeper shade may also need darkening – by the same basic streaking process – in order to enhance the solid appearance of the panel. Since this process requires a delicate touch and carefully measured amounts of paint on the brush, it may be a good idea to do a bit of practice on a white surface before committing oneself to a lot of work. Painted wood panelling is probably one of the few cases where a gloss or semi-gloss varnish

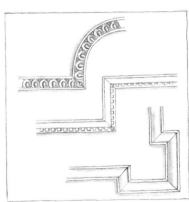

Top row, left to right: *The outline of a wooden panel. A pale, warm base colour which will later shine through. The basic form of the grain.*
Bottom row, left to right: *The darkening of parts in shade. The finished panel. A painted or dragged panel raised into a pyramid.* Above: *Various kinds of moulding with their shadows.*

105

Above: *The books and shelves are painted on a flat wall. So is the window. See how the latter appears to be recessed into the wall to make way for a painted plant pot on the window sill. The painted curtains match the real ones on the real windows.*
Opposite: *For the child with a storage problem, simple coloured compartments round the bedroom door can offer easy access to all his most treasured possessions.*

could be used.

A variation of the theme of panelling might consist of painted rather than wooden panels, perhaps with a shallow pyramid instead of a flat surface. This kind would be considerably quicker and easier to do as there would be no visible grain. We could even do a painted panel with a stippled or 'dragged' finish on it.

The principles of light and shade involved in painting panel mouldings can be applied to any kind of moulding to be painted around an area of wall, perhaps with a different colour within the enclosed area.

A gilt mirror can be a nice addition to a mural composition, or even just to fill an awkward or empty space. To paint this we must decide where the main viewing point would be and paint a suitable reflected image of what one would see if a real mirror were there. To paint the effect of gilt, cover the whole area occupied by the frame with a pale ochre containing a little brighter yellow, then darken down the areas not receiving light – from an appropriate light source – with a darker, slightly muddier version of this colour, making sure that the change in colour on curved surfaces has the rubbed look of gilt. Nooks and crannies in the design should then be darkened with a darker brown containing a tinge of greeny gold. Areas reflecting light should not be clear-cut as they would be if it were a truly shiny surface. The brightest reflecting areas should then be represented by white fringes on the golden surface, but these must have a fuzzy look like the rest.

In the kitchen of a house where I once painted a mural there was a small, shallow cupboard recessed into the wall on one side of the fireplace. It had leaded glass doors and contained a service of crockery. The owners had always been irritated by this architectural imbalance, and wanted 'the other' cupboard; so I painted one in the same position on the other side. In choosing the perspective for the inside surfaces of the cupboard I stood in the centre and reproduced what I could see in the real cupboard. In the absence of any real cupboard I would otherwise have chosen my perspective in the normal way from a suitable viewing point in the room in question.

If we have an area of wall which perhaps needs an ordinary painting, but we have no painting, we can simply paint one . . . on the wall of course! The same light and shade requirements must

Right: *A composite gilt mirror reflecting a room.* Far right: *A shallow cupboard set into the wall.*

 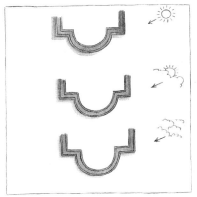 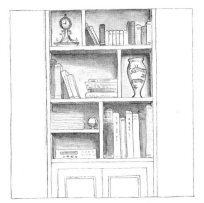

be considered for the illusion of a picture frame as for the moulding of our panel above, but in this case the strips of shadow cast by the frame – both on the wall and on the painting inside – are rather important. Narrow shadows of this kind on the edges of things are very important in mural painting. Their form and density depend partly on the shape of the thing casting the shadow, but also on the nature of the light received in the area.

A set of painted bookshelves interspersed with decorative and utilitarian items can always increase the intellectual and artistic atmosphere of the surroundings. Again, the inside geometry of the shelves must be decided in terms of the angle from which the painting is mainly going to be viewed. Note the inside shading of the bookshelves.

Far left: *Your nightcap, ma'am.* Left: *Shadows cast in different lights.* Above: *A painted library with ornaments and hi-fi.*

CHAPTER NINE

THE PAINTING OF
AN INDOOR MURAL

Every picture tells a story, but the painting of a picture also has a story to it. To complete the book we now have a description of the creation of an indoor mural in its various stages. This should help to put in perspective many of the points made individually in the preceding chapters.

Earlier in the book I described the various processes involved in painting an outdoor mural. I shall finally give an illustrated account of the painting of an indoor mural, this time in the main living room of a country house in Brazil! (Throughout this chapter you should refer to the photographs on pages 114 and 115).

I start by doing two initial sketches, each of them to be framed by the illusion of a large wooden window divided into three sections. One of the sketches consists of figures in a purely imaginary landscape with a river, hills and trees. The other is a romanticized extension of the garden which is actually visible, from the main viewing point of the picture, through a pair of broad french windows in the adjacent wall.

The latter subject is chosen. I now produce a scale drawing containing more exact colours and greater detail, which establishes the size of the imaginary window frame and its position on the wall. The size of the window is a compromise between the average size of other such windows in the building and the amount of space available for painting on. In fact it turns out to be very slightly on the small side, because I have to leave a decent margin of wall on either side. Height presents no problem. So, I measure the distance between the left-hand corner of the room and the plane of a long arch stretching out across the room from the right-hand side of my wall. I divide this in half to find the centre point, establish the natural height of the base of the window, and draw a horizontal straight line as the base of my window. I then draw uprights at either end and finish the contour by adding a shallow arch over the top with flattened-out ends, equal to the ones over the other windows.

We now have the outline of the window in place, and I have to draw more lines to represent the thickness of the window frame's facing surface, plus the two uprights dividing the window into three sections. Lines are also drawn to denote the inside surfaces of the window frame. Note that in this case these are all symmetrical, because the main viewing point of the picture is a group of chairs and sofas directly in front of the picture at the far end of the room. There is no parallax distortion as described in the section on windows in Chapter 5.

When the scale drawing is finished, I locate it on the wall using the common multiplier I first used to fit the drawing onto the paper, then scale it up using a suitable grid. Only the basic features of the scale drawing need to be pencilled in now.

I now step back and view the main feature of the garden through the real french windows, namely the low stone wall with railings on top. I draw imaginary lines with my eye to the point where the wall and railings would disappear at infinity, and make a point on the painting surface. This is the vanishing point. I then draw the relevant lines outwards to the left, and step back again. Do the lines of my imaginary wall and railings coincide with the real ones from the main viewing point? If not, I make the necessary adjustments until they are right. I then proceed to insert the main contours of the composition: the edge of the lawn and a line for each of the two sections of horizon – one depicting

Below: *A simple landscape with figures for the* trompe-l'œil *window.* Bottom: *A painted extension of the garden which is really there.*

dense tropical forest on the left, the other depicting distant hills above a lake on the right. An outline of the large tree in the centre is also introduced at this stage.

It is now time to choose the base colours and start to fill in the main colour masses of the painting. I like to get the whole surface covered with paint as soon as I can, to give an overall view of its compositional balance from the start, and to enable me to continue working on the whole thing simultaneously, rather than perfecting one part before moving on to the next. In this way any adjustments of balance that may be required can take place before a lot of detailed work has been done.

At this point I start to insert all the main details into the painting: densely wooded hills and a flowering forest on the left; the main structure of the railings on a more solid-looking wall; dark foliage beside the window on the left; details of grass in the foreground and shadows across the lawn; shrubs around the main tree; more details of the lake and distant landscape; and some wispy clouds which help to give a sense of depth to the composition and add a point of interest to a clear sky.

In painting the forest scene on the left-hand side of the painting, it is important to make sure that it contains as much variety of colour as possible within reason. In painting natural scenes there is always a danger of ending up with too much green and blue. This must be avoided. Groups of trees are not only green. Like rough grass, they contain a multitude of colours, and the effect of dark patches of shade seen at a distance is often a warm one. A certain amount of enhancement or exaggeration can be done when rendering these different hues in paint, but there is a point beyond which they start to look false and lose their attraction. Care must be taken not to pass this point.

At present the colours of the different trees are fairly crude, since we are still dealing with what I call base colours – they will be refined later. The effect of sunlight on trees is initially painted in rather solid shapes, in pale warm tones. Such areas of light are an important element in giving the trees their shape. Achieving the effect of brightness is always difficult, and white is the lightest colour we have. It is all right to use white on the bright part of painted window frames, but it appears very cold and artificial if used to represent light on natural objects. The brightness of these must generally be kept warm.

An interesting sense of depth and distance is created by the relative height and position of the trees. Remember, we must find that illusive 'sense of place', and the suggestion of openings in the forest and large areas of enclosed space – not necessarily visible – is a great help in achieving this. If the viewer can be led to imagine things which are not wholly visible in the painting but which are obviously there, the painting has partly succeeded in stimulating the desired emotional response.

Some of the painting appears to be quite rough and messy at this stage, because, although the basic layout has been estab-lished in the scale drawing, I am still experimenting a bit to find the most effective shape and relationship between the trees. The creative act does not end with the drawing – it is a process of

Below: *Positioning of the wall and railings is the main key to perspective in this case.* Bottom: *The main outlines are drawn in before painting commences.*

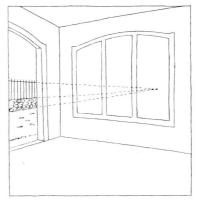

Above: *Outlines are transferred to the wall, and colour masses are filled in.* Right: *The forest grows. Light, shade, variety of colour and mass distribution are important. The garden wall and railing start to appear.* Below: *The wooden window frame takes shape, and landscape features are developed in the middle and far distance.*

Top: *The picture starts to look more substantial now, especially with the addition of the railings, clouds, and foliage by the window.* Centre: *The windows are drawn in and painted white. Wood tone and grain can now be built up in the same way as the window frame. Light and shade are painted on the glass.* Bottom: *The finished product, coinciding with the layout of the garden through the french window.*

refinement which continues throughout the work. There are no rules about how paintings have to be painted. In the end everyone adopts their own approach. Some artists put their paint on the surface in a brisk fashion, and cannot bear to touch it again. I am the opposite, since I work gradually at refining my images, which I believe is an appropriate way to tackle this kind of art. Yet even within my own system there is a degree of variation – if I paint something very quickly and it happens to turn out particularly well in its spontaneous form, I may well leave it, and work at incorporating other more refined parts of the work into what I have done. This is not the norm however. Experience teaches us how far to go, what to leave alone and what to work on, what is wrong with the work, and when it is finished – although at times I am tempted to believe that a work of art is never truly finished, only abandoned!

It is now time to build up the far distance on the right-hand side, choosing basic colours for the high wooded terrain on the horizon – later to be modified with various subtle tones. Here again the temptation may be to go instinctively for cold colours on the horizon. There is no doubt that distant landscape does tend towards bluish colours in reality, but any blues, greys, etc, we use to paint the shaded side of hills, vegetation and so on will be considerably enhanced by the slightly-warmer-than-real colours we use to compensate on the lit side of these masses. Care has to be taken not to make distant colours too vivid, or they will lose their atmospheric feel of distance. Pale pinks, ochres and yellows can be combined effectively to render illuminated distant terrain. Vestigial lines of trees on or near the horizon will add interest and provide miniature focal points which generally help the painting. Again, any predominance of cool colours in the shaded areas of the far distance can be slightly modified by an addition of purples and browns – but such hues in shade should be kept within a fairly narrow spectrum.

I paint in the two dense masses of vegetation in the middle distance and a sunlit valley between them leading down to the lake. A grand building provides a focal point of interest in the valley. On the near side of the lake a grassy headland with a coppice lies in shade beyond the end of the garden. Here again I try to achieve my beloved 'sense of place', and by putting the sunlit valley in the distance I am trying to make use of another useful phenomenon: a 'way out' of the picture on the far side. This valley leads we know not where, but it makes us wonder. Such things as these invariably add to the interest and romantic atmosphere of a painting.

I am also gradually building up the wooden texture of the window frame all the time – basically using the same process as the one described for wooden panelling in Chapter 8 – and putting in light and shade on the inside surfaces of the frame. Note the richness of texture and deep red colouring of the Brazilian hardwood used for building in that part of the world.

Now it is time to work on the texture of the stones in the wall – which must resemble the real stones in the garden as closely as possible – and add some deeper shadows denoting strong sunlight. I also start to develop the intricate wrought-iron railings as a continuation of those existing in the garden itself.

At this point I draw in the two open windows and paint the areas they occupy in white. This is because I want to start the process of building up the wood texture in the same way as for the window frame, i.e. with a pale reddish wood tone to start with on the white wall. If we can still have its lightness shining through when we have applied all our other coats of wood texture, then the painted wood will appear to have the depth it has in reality. The scenery is clearly visible through the left-hand window, whereas the right-hand one is wider open to give a good view of the lake and distant landscape, unimpeded by the window. Yet the landscape on the right is still there to be espied through the cracks. The left-hand window panes have a slight haze on them to give the impression of glass, and the reflections of cloud and foliage are clearly visible at the top.

I develop light, shade and tone in the foliage on the main tree and on its trunk and branches. And see how the grass has grown! The dark shadows of other trees across the lawn serve to enhance the sense of space in strong sunlight.

All the lights and shades, hinges and handles are added to the windows. The wood has now been given its final treatment to create the appearance of deep rich texture and strong graining, not to forget the carpenter's joints and the round wooden pins which appear flush with the surface. The scenery and vegetation has all been toned, variegated and harmonized with its surroundings, and finally those important little shadows have been painted round the outside of the window frame, where it must appear to be standing out from the wall. In short, the work is finished.

EPILOGUE

The serious mural painter must be like a criminal – leave no trace of the job he has done, except for the job itself, and always return to the scene of the crime. And since most criminals end up in Brazil, what better subject for a mural painting than a nice Brazilian scene!

118

Anyone who has read this book will know that mural painting is a wide subject. None of the information contained in the book was learned in schools – it was picked up on the job. My experience of painting murals has been one of trial and error, and I hope that this fact will give heart to those who wish to try for themselves.

The examples of work and ideas for subject matter described in the various chapters were taken mainly from the jobs I have done, which in most cases consisted of my own interpretations of the clients' taste. My aim in writing the book was not to dictate a certain taste and style to other people, nor to tell anyone what to paint. It was really to give an initial impetus to the aspiring artist. I have provided what you might call a framework of possibilities to be built on and developed in an individual way.

I was an amateur painter for years before I ever did a mural. I always knew I wanted to paint, but for much of the time I had no clear idea why I wanted to paint, nor indeed what I should paint. What was the value of this pastime I was engaged in, if it had any value at all? The answer began to come not through some miraculous artistic vision, but from the simple fact that in painting murals I suddenly had before me a specific task which required a bit of thought and some careful preparation. This was a refreshing change from just dreaming up arbitrary subjects to paint on canvas, hoping I might sell them. I therefore hope that the words and pictures in my book will motivate other people in the same position.

I was in fact taken by surprise when a lady asked me at a party if I would care to paint a mural on the wall at the end of her town garden. As far as I could remember, the idea had never occurred to me. I hadn't the slightest idea how I should go about it. So I simply bought a pad of paper and some pencils, drew the approximate outline of the wall on all the pages, and started making sketches of everything I could think of. There were about twenty drawings – a number I have never repeated since! Some of them were completely dotty – one of them was even called 'Cornish Pastiche'! But between the two of us we managed to choose a drawing, made certain modifications, added a number of features from the other drawings, and behold . . . there was our subject. A scale drawing was prepared.

I was drawn to the wall, which was a large wall. It had a hold on me. I was not in the least concerned about my ability to complete my first job on a grand scale, and this surprised me. The size and momentum of the job were such that I simply became absorbed in what I was doing. The prospect of my finished painting swam warm in my eyes as I approached it day by day, and I was driven on. But I began to realize at a certain point that it was a two-way process. The more the work proceeded, the more I found that I was influenced by the growing picture in the way I did it. The picture stood before me, and it was getting stronger. It was almost as if it were gaining its own momentum – finding a personality of its own. There were even moments when I wondered – absurdly – if my work of art was not in fact a pre-existing thing – a potential which had always been in that place – but which had merely required a suitable agent to bring it into being.

Painting a picture on a large scale was an exciting process. The affective power which I put into my work was transferred to the picture – locked into the wall as it were – and I was pleased to think that it would remain there. It was going to become a source of affective power – an endless supply of the energy of my own affection radiating to the ones who viewed it.

The mental and physical effort required in painting a mural, and of applying oneself in a particular situation, can have the effect of clearing the head and bringing one down to earth – hopefully not head-first from the ladder! This is what happened to me. It made me approach my work from a new angle. I suddenly found that I had to apply objective criteria to such questions as composition and the choice of subject matter. For years I had been in the habit of looking into myself to find a source of inspiration, and was often frustrated because there was apparently nothing there!

But in order to paint a mural the initial impulse had to come from the things about me. As a result I am happily no longer subject to the whims of 'inspiration' in the same way as before. The proverbial inspiration – or what I would describe as a surge of enthusiasm to develop the germ of a new idea – does still come into the picture, but not in a dominant way. Its frequent absence at the start of a project is no longer able to block the creative process. Instead it is like a resource to be drawn on in a process which has already been mapped out.

Murals have a strange attraction which is hard to pin-point. People are fascinated by them. Throughout history the mural has probably been the most vital and formative kind of pictorial art, until modern times at least. To me, the painting of walls has become the most vivid and colourful manifestation of the fact that the human brain can go beyond its immediate situation – the world of knowledge through sensory perception – into an imaginary state of being of its own creation. The walled room or the walled garden – *hortus conclusus* – are the most obvious boundaries of the immediate, sensory world we live in. Everything in the room is certain. But the certainty ends at the blank wall. What is beyond the wall? Or what could lie beyond the wall? Almost anything we care to put there. But we have to be careful. An artist painting on canvas certainly has a much wider choice, and is truly freer to paint whatever he likes – he can always turn the canvas round and lean it against the wall. But in painting a mural we are conditioned to some extent by the fact that our work is really going to be a part of the world we live in. Just as the stage designer has to match his backdrop to the words of the drama, we have to match our painting to the life we lead, or would like to lead, which is not a drama but could possibly be a little more dramatic.

Perhaps we should learn a lesson from the cavemen, who were the first artists, and try to believe that the paintings on our walls will do for us in a modern sense what they hoped it would do for them . . . bring fortune in hunting and fertility to the herds!

APPENDIX

PITFALLS TO BE AVOIDED AND OTHER PRACTICAL HINTS

1 Condition of surface

Make sure that your painting surface is in good condition before you start. Internal dampness is to be avoided at all costs. New plaster should be thoroughly dry before you start.

2 Priming the surface

Make sure you use the right primer. If for any reason you are unsure about the surface, do a small test with your paints and scratch it carefully with a screwdriver when dry – the paint should not come off. Avoid painting on eggshell or other shiny finishes, unless they have been very thoroughly sanded indeed, and preferably re-primed.

3 Use of tools

Remember that all tools can be dangerous, especially electrical ones. Make sure you know how to use them, that they are in good condition, and that they are kept away from children. Avoid the accidental ingestion of paints and all chemical substances. Always wash hands well after using such materials. Keep them out of reach of children, not only for their sakes, but also to protect your home. Young children tend to be 'great artists'.

4 Use of ladders, etc.

If you are up a ladder or working on a platform, remember at all times where you are. Please . . . don't step backwards. I did once, and had a very lucky escape! Check all structures regularly for stability.

5 Protection of surfaces

Cover the floor well with groundsheets, old bed linen, polythene sheeting, or newspaper. Put a strip of masking tape along the top of skirting boards, etc., so that it sticks out a bit. This will avoid a lot of tedious chipping away at paint spots later.

6 Drawing materials

Avoid using felt pens and magic markers on the wall. They normally contain tenacious dyes which show through many layers of paint.

7 Pencil lines

Always draw as lightly and carefully as possible in pencil. Heavy pencil lines can show through paint and are difficult to conceal.

8 Checking perspective, etc.

Check the effects of your perspective and parallax carefully and frequently while drawing on the wall. What looks perfect on paper can sometimes play tricks on the eye when scaled up on the wall, and minor adjustments may be required. The appearance of your work from the main viewing point is crucial, but other important viewing points should be taken into account where possible in making decisions about perspective and parallax.

9 Balance of composition

Check the overall balance of your composition carefully when putting in the main colour masses for the first time. Its various components will react with one another when they start to take shape and, once again, what looked good on paper may require a little modification on the larger scale. I have never fully understood the reason for this, but it is certainly worth spotting incongruities at an early stage in order to avoid wasting valuable effort.

10 Gradated sky

When painting a large area of gradated sky, it is best to mix a substantial quantity of the deeper blue required at the top – in a jam jar or a plastic cup for example – and cover the upper part using say a 3cm (1in) decorator's brush. Then decant a part of the remaining paint into another container and add a suitable amount of white, but not too much, and stir it up. The next layer of paler blue is now applied, leaving a 'tidemark' between the two shades. This mark is eliminated by brushing across it carefully in many vertical strokes – continuously – to give a tight zigzag pattern. This should yield an intermediate shade where the two have mixed. If some of the upper layer has already dried, we still have some of that paint left to apply again for blending on the surface with the paler shade. If the change in shade is still too abrupt when the paint dries, we can make a new shade from the two we already have to modify the intermediate zone. This process can be repeated all the way down, through white to a golden sunset at the bottom. We are dealing with very fine gradations of colour when painting sky, and a certain amount of trial and error may be required. But as a general rule it is best to mix enough colour so that we always have some of the previous colour left to make corrections. When painting a smaller area of sky, it is not normally necessary to be quite so systematic.

11 Work order

The prospect of painting a large surface may be daunting, especially in the early stages when it is all messy and unfinished. There may be times when you feel there is so much to do that you don't know where to start. This can be depressing. I normally resolve the problem by mentally dividing the picture up into its natural components, and working on them in rotation. For example: sky, grass, masonry, distant landscape, water, foliage, figures etc., etc. I firmly believe in developing the picture as a whole rather than concentrating exclusively on one part at a time. When I arrive at work in the morning, I almost invariably sit down for a while and decide which 'sections' I am going to work on in the course of the day, and in what order. I then exclude the rest from my thoughts for the time being, and work only on those.

12 Working mobility

When using ladders or platforms, I attach great importance to retaining as much mobility as possible over the whole wall at all times. For this reason I always try to get a light aluminium step-ladder, which is easy to lift, or have a mobile scaffolding tower on wheels, unless the terrain makes a static scaffolding essential. In the case of the latter, it must of course be erected so as to offer easy – and most important safe – access to all parts of the surface. When painting on ceilings I never lie down. Working on my back would be very restricting. I always stand. Working above your head is a bit hard on the arm and neck at first, but after a little while the arm muscles compensate and the position starts to feel more natural. And though it is indeed more difficult working in this position, it is very good practice to work without having anything to rest your hand on. There is nothing quite like a ceiling to give the artist a steady hand!

13 Difficulty of access

Two parts of the wall are always hard to paint on, and it is prudent to avoid placing any highly complex images in these zones. For a right-handed person, one of these is the area close to a corner on the left-hand side. This is because the body gets in the way and the painting hand – in this case the right – has to pass across the body and then do a 'right turn', so to speak, before it can work on the wall. Trying to turn the body to get it out of the way doesn't seem to help. I am left-handed, so I have the same problem when working in right-hand corners. The other difficult area, which affects everyone, is the part of the wall close to the floor. If we crouch or kneel down and try to work with a lowered hand, the contorted position of the hand and arm make it difficult to control the movements of the brush. If we lie down and try to work with our elbows on the ground, the hand and forearm will have a rather limited radius of movement, thus impeding our effort. So – try to keep the contents of these areas fairly simple if you can.

14 Light switches, etc.

Most walls contain light switches and plug holes. Occasionally I have tried to paint over them, if the material they were made of would take the paint. But on the whole I have decided that this is not a good idea. The result tends to be messy, and the appliance in question is still visible. If anything it looks worse than before. In certain cases it is possible to minimize their presence by surrounding them with dense imagery such as foliage, rather than leaving them isolated in the middle of, say, an area of sea or sky.

15 Glazing technique

Try to glaze the finished work on a fairly dry, windy day if possible, with an open window. Acrylic matt glaze – available in sizeable containers from good builders merchants – dries at the same speed as water, but there is a lot of liquid around during this operation, and quicker drying can help to give a cleaner result and minimize dripping. This kind of glaze sometimes looks slightly milky and opaque when first put on to the surface. It is always a bit frightening to see your work temporarily go blurred, but it dries clear and invisible. Start at the top and work across the painting, doing one suitably-sized square at a time. A wide decorator's brush is best, and it is important not to get too much glaze on it at a time, or it will splash around and tend to run down the wall. Attempt to cover the wall evenly and thoroughly with glaze. If at any time you are not sure which parts have been glazed and which have not, look at the painting obliquely against the light and you will see the shine of the wet glaze reflecting the light. The shiny wet glaze may make the gradated areas of the painting look a bit rough and irregular, since shiny surfaces have the effect of heightening and exaggerating colour differences, but it will all return to normal when dry. If the rest of the room is decorated in silky or eggshell finishes, a mixture of acrylic gloss and matt glazes may be used. In this case it is best to make a substantial quantity of this mixture then do a test strip to match the finish with that of the rest of the room. Then add a little more of one or the other to achieve the correct degree of silkiness if necessary. As a general rule I like to avoid giving my works too glossy a finish, as this would introduce the problem of light reflection and glare. Outdoor murals may require a slightly glossier finish depending on circumstances, because by its nature this will offer a more perfect seal against the elements. All photographs of the work should be taken before application of any final coat containing elements of gloss. Glare causes havoc in photographs.

16 Artificial lighting

In an ill-lit environment the work may greatly benefit from some special lighting. This can perhaps be cleverly done by the positioning of standard lamps, etc., but many of my works have been specially lit with floodlights – possibly masked to illuminate the exact area of the painting – or with a combination of floodlight to illuminate the whole work, and spotlight to enhance the illumination of bright parts of the work such as sky with lit clouds or a sunset. Specialized lighting should be carefully positioned to avoid accidentally dazzling the occupants of the area in question.

ACKNOWLEDGMENTS

John and Isabel Murphy; Jeremy and Britta Lloyd; George and Susan Parker; Michael and Daisy Orchant; Stephen and Barbara Lee; Roger and Denise Poulter; Terence Edgar; Robert and Sandi Lacey; Marjorie McKean; Paul and Gillian Friedman; Stephen and Yolanda Plant; Ignacius and Gina Lidonni; Roddy Llewellyn; Alfonsus and Margaret Kelly; Nigel and Ann Wallis; Maurice and Evelyn Hope; Paul Hargreaves; Barbara Leedham; Lorraine Johnston; Agnaldo and Lucilia de Oliveira; Levi Agiar Nunes; Athos and Adelina Pisoni; The Viscount of Rio Claro; Richard Compton-Miller; Marlen Bovell; Patricia Cheston-Porter; Mario Venturi; Franco and Marcella Ventura; Jamie Garnock; Timothy and Sarah Von Halle; The Prince and Princess Tortorici di Raffadali.

I would like to thank all these people, as well as my family and friends, for the important part they played in the development of my career as a working artist.

INDEX

Page numbers in italics refer to illustrations

abstract compositions 89
acrylic paints 49-51
alcoves 32, 65
animals 53, 97-101
    horses 53
    mythical creatures 100
    pets 100
arches 21, 28, 29, 53-6, 62-4
Assisi School 10-11
awnings 72-3

balconies 65-6
balustrades 69
Baroque murals 12-13
bathrooms 36
bedrooms 25, 33, 36, 98
birds 37, 79, 98-100
bookshelves 107, 109
bridges 84
brushes 52
buildings 77, 84, 86-8
Byzantine art 10

cave painting 8-9
ceiling painting 12, 13, 24-5, 36-7, 124
children's rooms 33, 106
classical subjects 36
cloth 71-3
clothing 96-7
clouds 85-6
colour
    in far distance 76, 78, 81, 116
    in foreground 81-3
    in sky 84-6
    in stone 53, 57, 64, 68-9
    of trees 80, 82-3, 113, 116
    of water 78, 80
    of wood 104-05, 116-17
columns 70
commedia dell'arte 97
composition, balance of 53, 123
conservatories 21, 32
Coypel, Antoine 13
cupboards 24, 108
curtains 24, 71-2

da Cortona, Pietro 12
difficult areas, for painting 124
dining room 33
distance, colour in 76, 78-81, 113, 116
distance, far 52, 76, 116
distance, middle 53, 76-81, 116
domes, illusion of 25, 25, 87
doors and doorways 21
drapes 73
drawing and painting materials 40-1, 42, 49-52, 122
drawings 40-4

Egyptian murals 9
electrical fittings 124-5
Etruscan murals 9

fabrics 71-3
faces 93-5
Ferrara School 12
fish 101
Florence, Brancacci Chapel 11
foliage 80-1, 82-4, 113, 117
foreground 81-4
    buildings in 86-8
french windows 21, 36

garden walls 30
gardens 28-9, 30
gateways 30
Giotto 10-11
glass 61-2, 117
glazing 125
grass 81-2
gravel 81
grid, use of
    on scale drawing 44
    on wall 48-9

halls 36, 66
horizon 76, 116
human figure 16, 33, 92-7
    body positions 92-3
    clothes 96-7
    eyes 94
    facial expressions 93-5
    hair 96
    mouths 94-5
    pairs or groups 96
humour 101

indoor mural painting 32-7, 45
    process described 112-17
inspiration 121

ladders 37, 49, 122, 124
landings 22, 36, 87
landscapes 28-9, 74-84
Leonardo da Vinci 12, 100-01
    Battle of Anghiari 12, 100-01
light, reflected 61-2, 108
light and shade 52, 56, 61-2, 68, 69, 70, 71, 73, 80, 82, 83, 108, 117
    back light 69, 70, 83
light source 60-2, 64, 66, 69, 70, 73, 104
light switches 124-5
lighting, special 125
living rooms 32
loo, murals in 36, 83

Mantegna, Andrea 12
Mantua 12
Masaccio 11-12
measuring 44, 48

Michelangelo 12
middle distance 53, 76-81, 116
mirrors 108
mobility, importance of when painting 124
movement, sense of
    in fabrics 72
    in grass 82
    in water 78-9
    introduced by animals 101
Muybridge, Edward 97

oil paints 49, 51
openings in walls 21
    see also arches; windows
oriental themes 66, 84
outdoor mural painting 28-32
    process described 40-57
outlines, transferring to wall 49

painting surface, preparation of 44-5, 122
paints 49-51, 85
panelling 104-08
paper, types of 40-1
passageways 36
    views across 29-30
pathetic fallacy 100
patios 30
patronage, key factor in mural painting 13
patterns 88
perspective 56, 72, 108, 123
pets 100
pictures 108-09
plants and flowers 23, 32, 33
Pompeii, 10, 18
priming 45, 122
protection of surfaces 122

railings 65-6
Raphael 12
Renaissance murals 10-12
roads 77
rocks 84
    see also stone
Rococo murals 13
Roman murals 9-10
Rubens, Peter Paul 100

safety 45, 49, 122
scale drawings 44
shadows 24, 66, 81, 109, 117
    see also light and shade
sketches 38-9, 40-3
sky 25, 30, 37, 52, 84-6, 123
sports areas 32
steps 69-70
stone 53, 56-7, 64, 68-9, 84
subjects
    indoor 32-37
    outdoor 28-32
sunsets 86

surrealistic compositions 17, *43*, 88
swimming pools 32

terraces 68-9
Tiepolo, Giovanni Battista 13
trompe l'oeil
   Baroque 12-13
   Renaissance 12
   Roman 10
trompe l'oeil devices

on ceilings 24-5, 36-7
as extensions of space 21
as openings 21, 28, 29, 60-2, 112-17
as structure beyond wall 21
this side of wall 21-4, 104-09

varnishes 51-2, 105
Vatican, murals in 12
Venetian School 13
Versailles 13

wall, preparation of 44-5, 122
wardrobes, built-in *25*, 33, 98
water 77-80, 84, 99
watercolours 42
well, of house 29-30
wind, *see* movement, sense of
windows 21, 28, 60-2, 112-17
wood 104-08, 116-17
woods, *see* trees
work, order of 123